DEDICATION:

This book is dedicated to my grandmother, Patricia Louise Ross Pace, who devoted her life to the education of children, foreign and domestic, of Hopewell, Virginia; to my grandfather, Thompson Gardenhire Pace Sr., my mother, Martha Sue Pace Traylor; and my father, William Ellsworth Traylor Sr. It is also dedicated to the past employees of Mrs. Pace's Kindergarten and Nursery and Hopewell School of Childhood, and especially to the extended Pace and Traylor families.

Mrs. Pace's Nursery and Kindergarten school was the oldest licensed "CDC" (Children Day Care) center in Hopewell and second to none in the State of Virginia, licensed in 1948.

I wish to thank several people who helped to make this book possible. I am grateful for the help of many staff members and former students of Pace's Kindergarten, who generously shared their wisdom and their memories of attending and working for the school.

Special thanks:

—to my friend Joyce Pritchard, who with great personal sacrifice for over a year, inspired the idea for this book.

—to my brother Bill Traylor for his constant love, interest, insights, professional competence, project leadership and for his many excellent suggestions.

—to Virginia "Diddy" Ford Flannagan for her invaluable school play editing and production writing assistance, for her inner commitment to the material, and for her skill, sensitivity, and care in fulfilling that commitment. Her life of integrity and service has supported my many travels and involvements outside the home. It's easy to teach the principles that your loved ones live.

—Thompson Gardenhire Pace, III for his part in my journey. He has been more than a mentor, guide, and philosopher!

—to Chris Wiegard for his editing leadership, support and encouragement to finalize this book.

Proofreaders: Edna Marie Traylor, Kathy Podlewski, Ralph McLean Angell B.A. University of Richmond; M.A. Duke University.

This book is about an important part of Hopewell's rich history, Hopewell's First Day-Care Center. The kindergarten was founded in 1941 by my grandmother Patricia Louise Ross Pace. The book covers the founding and operation of the school from 1941 until its doors closed in 1986.

The book contains many class teachers' portraits and pictures of the annual performances that Mrs. Pace took such pleasure in producing. Fortunately, many photographs are available as my father was a devoted photographer and the school was featured often in the local newspaper.

This book will be an important addition to the existing documentation of Hopewell's rich historical past. It will be appreciated by the School's alumni, but also by the many relatively new arrivals in our community in our 400th anniversary. It demonstrates and explains in simple language the intricacies involved in providing a sound foundation to the education of many of Hopewell's current and past leaders, community members and business owners.

The impact Mrs. Pace and the kindergarten have had on Hopewell will be apparent throughout the book. In fact, you will recognize the logos of many prominent Hopewell businesses I have included in a special section.

I have worked for several years to collect photographs and commentary from a variety of sources. It has indeed been a labor of love and also, a privilege to work with many of her former students as I researched the schools history.

TABLE OF CONTENTS:

CITY POINT—HOPEWELL, VIRGINIA

Mrs. Pace's Kindergarten & Nursery School 1941 - 1986
Hopewell's First Children's Day Care Center

MRS. PACE'S KINDERGARTEN
AND NURSERY SCHOOL

RHYTHM BAND, DANCING, SPATTER PAINTING
CREATIVE ART, PROGRESSIVE PRE SCHOOL TRAINING
TRAINED SUPERVISION

BROWN APT.   OPPOSITE
CITY POINT   CITY POINT INN

6

Mrs. Patricia Pace moved to City Point in 1915. She and her husband, Thompson G. Pace Sr., had two children, Thompson Pace, Jr. and Martha Sue Pace (Traylor). Mrs. Pace, a graduate of North Carolina's Lenoir-Rhyne College in 1909, opened Hopewell's first day care center in 1941. The facility, located in the Brown apartment building, offered nursery and kindergarten instruction to youngsters 3 to 5 years old. Mrs. Pace continued and was joined by her daughter, Sue, in 1953. In 1958 the entire school moved to 519 Appomattox Street. It was renamed "Hopewell School of Childhood." Mrs. Pace continued running the school until her death in 1961. Mrs. Traylor then ran the school until she retired in 1986. Mrs. Pace gave thousands of Hopewell children many fond memories of her schools; swinging on the swings, snacking on milk and butter cookies (which had a hole in the middle and could be nibbled, wearing them on their fingers) rhythm band, and the glorious end of the school year musical play productions, starring all of the students.

Thompson Gardenhire Pace Sr.—1902

Thompson Gardenhire Pace Jr., Patricia Leigh Ross Pace,
Thompson Gardenhire Pace Sr. 1916

Great Grandfather—Richard Ross and Children—Behind Great Grandfather to left—Aunt Onnie Barker—Uncle Ben Ross, Patrice Leigh Ross Pace—Aunt Easter Ritchie—Uncle Charles Ross—Uncle Dr. Edward Ross MD.

TUBIZE ARTIFICIAL SILK COMPANY OF AMERICA

Thomas G. Pace Sr.

A native of Trenton Georgia, he resides in Hopewell since 1915, and is active in civic and fraternal circles. He is a chancellor of Hopewell Lodge, 141 Knights of the Pythians, an active member of the Hopewell Aerie Fraternal Order of Eagles, and of the First Methodist Church. Tom had one brother, Jerry C. Pace of Trenton, Ga.

TUBIZE CHATILLON CORPORATION

ON THE FIRST DAY OF OCTOBER, NINETEEN HUNDRED
AND THIRTY, THESE MEN AND WOMEN COMPLETED
FIVE OR TEN-YEAR PERIODS OR MORE, IN THE EMPLOY
OF THIS COMPANY.

IN RECOGNITION OF THEIR LOYAL, EFFICIENT, AND
CONTINUOUS SERVICE, THEIR NAMES ARE INSCRIBED
ON THIS

Roll of Honor
Ten Year Service Record

LABOR
Moseley, H. E. .... June 16, '20

MAINTENANCE
Brewer, W. J. .... Sept. 21, '20
Campbell, Henry A. Aug. 16, '20
Cook, Henry D. .... Sept. 27, '20
Cook, N. H. .... Sept. 28, '20
Defibaugh, J. H. .... Sept. 20, '20
Franklin, W. E. .... Sept. 8, '20
Hammond, Fred E. .... June 30, '20
Harrison, Ed. C., Jr. Sept. 8, '20
Mifka, William D. Sept. 17, '20
Pace, Thomas .... Sept. 7, '20

Pepper, John E. .... Sept. 17, '20
Quick, Charles .... Sept. 21, '20
Rawlings, E. R. .... July 6, '20
Riddle, Charles T. .... Sept. 27, '20
Rogerson, W. E. .... Sept. 8, '20

NITRATING
Swann, Edwin V. .... Sept. 11, '20

ROME WORKS
Gibbons, H. H. .... Sept. 14, '20
Livingston, W. B. .... Sept. 23, '20

SERVICE
Clark, Harvey .... Sept. 20, '20
Deathe, Charles .... Sept. 7, '20

Five Year Service Record

DENITRATION
Carter, Thomas H. .. Sept. 11, '25
Ogles, William C. .... Sept. 9, '25
White, Allen S. .... Sept. 7, '25

FINISHING
Duke, Thurman A. .. Sept. 7, '25
Hughes, Charles F. Sept. 29, '25
Williams, May .... Sept. 14, '25

LABORATORY
Archer, E. G. .... Sept. 7, '25
Dolmetsch, C. .... Sept. 8, '25

MAINTENANCE
Bussart, Sell .... Sept. 17, '25

SERVICE
Dorris, Paul .... Sept. 18, '25

SKEINING
Combes, Mary .... Sept. 8, '25
Compton, Ira F. .... Sept. 4, '25
Harper, Willie .... Sept. 29, '25
Lockett, Woody .... Sept. 1, '25

Mazzie, Lottie .... Sept. 12, '25
McCann, Samuel .... Sept. 15, '25
Pelter, Frances .... Sept. 9, '25
Ratliff, Ethel .... Sept. 28, '25
Wells, Grace .... Sept. 22, '25
Wicker, Wilber .... Sept. 14, '25

SPINNING
Jackson, Tyree .... Sept. 14, '25
Melka, Emma .... Sept. 14, '25

SULPHYDRATE
Powell, Russell ...... Sept. 14, '25

TWISTING
Blount, Tennie .... Sept. 28, '25
Griffith, John A. .... Sept. 30, '25
Thacker, Henry P. .. Sept. 9, '25

ACID CONCENTRATION
(Colored)
Jones, Norfleet .... Sept. 1, '25

COLLODION MIX
(Colored)
Tucker, Alvin .... Sept. 7, '25

Published for and Edited by Employees
of Tubize Chatillon Corporation

TUBIZE DINNER

It's the CHARDONIZE YARN that gives so many "petal fabrics"

their creamy chalky bloom

● Dull, duller, dullest—gaily the new knitted cloths sweep into the dress market. It's a fashion stampede—and the very heart of it is Chardonize dull lustre yarn. For Chardonize gives certain unique and desirable qualities to fabrics of the angel skin and suede-surface types.

● Because of Chardonize, whose very dull, rich lustre is permanent, dresses of these fabrics can be tubbed again and again as long as they last without losing their fashion-perfect "petal" bloom.

● Because of Chardonize, their soft, suedelike hand remains permanently unimpaired.

● Because of Chardonize, these new dull dress fabrics have not required the "delustering" or "additional finishing" that so often result in limited serviceability.

● You'll be safe if you remember, when it comes to this season's dull-knit fabrics: *It's in the yarn.*

It's in the yarn

Sources of supply of fabrics or dresses will be furnished promptly on request.

TUBIZE·CHATILLON CORPORATION
2 PARK AVENUE · NEW YORK
MAKERS OF VISCOSE, NITROCELLULOSE AND ACETATE YARNS

14

The DuPont Guncotton Plant at Hopewell
BY G. C. RUFFIN

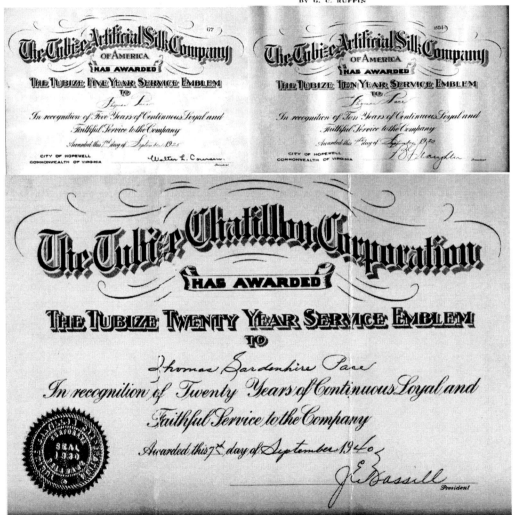

The Tubize Spinnerelle

I was trying to tell Tom what a wonderful thing it was for my friend Slim Lindbergh, to fly from New York to Paris on the "Spirit of St. Louis," Tom says he does not see anything about that to get drunk about, for he made this same trip on a mule named "Spirits of North Carolina," and did not get a cent for it, for he only went after a baseball that he had knocked over there. Says he would be playing baseball today if the factories could make 'em as fast as he could lose them. Says his bunts goes further than Babe Ruth's home runs. The last game he played in, he hit a ball in Durham and it killed tow bootleggers in Charlotte. Says, the best thing he has seen lately was little boy lifting two thousand pounds at the Collodion Calamities show, but that he had a little brother the same size, who lifted one end of a brick jail high enough for him to crawl out. Tom says he is worried blue with letters, telegrams, etc., from Hoover "Cal," and the Governor of North Carolina asking for advice. Says he will send Levi To straighten the Mississippi; Ed to China to settle the Laundry War, (he thinks Ed is the man for the job for if you did not know positively the Ed was born in North Carolina you would swear he was a china man); Tom will relieve the Governor while he takes his vacation. The first time he met Tom was at Ameen's corner where the "meal book Sheiks" congregate. I never saw such a face. You couldn't tell whether he was laughing or crying. He had on the remaining remains of a "seersucker suit," one gumboot, and a slipper; a go-to-thunder-hat with holes in it larger than the hat. Look at him now; orders his clothes direct from Sears & Roebuck; wears his badge for a star-pin; uses perfume and has his clothes done at Rainey's Laundry. He says the only objection he has to working for the company is that he cannot watch the ladies come in both gates at the same time. Says that if the ladies wear their skirts any shorter, all the men will be humpbacked. When he was a boy it took 37 yards of calico, 3 cards of hooks and eyes, 18 yards of lace, 6 spools of thread and 4 days to make a dress. Now they order a sample make an evening gown, and use what's left for a pocket handkerchief. If you want to know what is—ask Tom?

Massey and Pace with Plumbing Squad
TUBIZE NEVER-FAIL SPARK PLUGS

By Wade Epperson

With grimy hands and smiling grace,
The pipefitter you'll always find a place,
In rain or snow or sleet or wind,
He covers his face with a fur-lined grin,
On a rainy day, he can be gay,
On an outside job and he calls it "play."

The history of the Pipe Department dates back to the time when "Ed" Massey and Tom Pace screwed flanges on cocoanuts and threw them at each other and goes to the present date. For obvious reasons we will consider only the present.

Tom Pace (often eulogized by Col. Moseley) is evidently taking Mr. Roark's measure for a hat. If he runs true to form, Mr. Roark's hat will be two or three sizes too large or too small. Tom goes down to North Carolina ever so often to put double sockets on his beet stalks in order to get two beets to a plant.

T. G. Pace spent the holidays with his family in New London, N.C. He says they even have new Fords there.

1940 United States Federal Census for Thomas G Pace

					Name	Relation	Sex	Race	Age	Marital			Birthplace		Residence 1935
11	304	75	R	35	No	MEYERS Earl G	Head	M	W	5V	M	No R-4	KANSAS		Same
12						— Edith	Wife	F	W	53	M	No R-2	OHIO		Same
13						— George A (18)	Son	M	W	19	S	C-1	VIRGINIA		Same
14						— Harrold R	Son	M	W	18	S	H-3	VIRGINIA		Same
15	302	26	O	4500	No	Howell Francis M	Head	M	W	63	M	No R-4	London England		Same
16						— Bertha	Wife	F	W	56	M	No H-4	London England		Same
17	208	V8	O	7500	No	PACE Thomas G. Sr	Head	M	W	5V	M	No H-4	Georgia		Same
18						— Louise P.	Wife	F	W	50	M	No R-2	NORTH CAROLINA		Same
19						— Sue	Daughter	F	W	Vo	S	No H-4	VIRGINIA		Same

No		No	No No No	H						0	No
No	44	- - - -	40	PLUMING STEAM FITTING	SILK PLANT	PW				1200	No
	44 No No No	H	20	EDUCATION					0	800	No
	44	- - - -	16	TELEGRAPH	WESTERN UNION	PW			0	0	No

Year Income

Thomas G. Pace has purchased one of Henry's sport roadsters.

18

Hopewell Day by Day

Look at Tom Pace! I have seen him work for days trying to put a six-inch pipe in a four-inch hole—happy, contented and satisfied.

Tom Pace: When I sing I get tears in my eyes. What can I do for this? Answer: Stuff cotton in your ears.

Tom Pace wanted to sing a solo, but the committee decided the bridge wouldn't stand for it.

Tom Pace told me he planted one peck of confetti and sold Fourteen Hundred Dollars worth of paper flowers!

Pipe Department

Tom Pace has again taken his semiannual trip to his beet fields in North Carolina. He was provided with data for this flight by Colonel Moseley.

Ed Massey and Tom Pace undisputed sovereigns of the Chemical and Textile Areas, respectively are reported to be using advance guards and disguises when venturing into each other's territory.

Mr. Thomas G. Pace, the Pipe Department star entrant in the famous prevarication contest, was a Santa Claus visitor to his home town on a pre-Christmas visit.

T. G. Pace and family are now residing on Fifteenth Avenue, his family having moved here from New London, N.C. recently.

Thompson Gardenhire Pace, Jr., and Martha Sue Pace

1931

*Matha Sue, daughter of T. G. Pace, of M6
Department, with her famous cat, "Buddy,"
in bulldog attire.*

America's Greatest
Industrial Opportunity

HOPEWELL
VIRGINIA

AMERICA'S GREATEST
INDUSTRIAL OPPORTUNITY

HOPEWELL
VIRGINIA

DU PONT CHEMICAL COMPANY
INCORPORATED
WILMINGTON, DELAWARE

Hopewell, Va., America's Greatest Industrial Opportunity

DOMINATING FACTOR in winning the war, the city of Hopewell is rapidly becoming a dominating factor in winning the world's markets. Selected for the location of the world's largest guncotton factory, the original munitions base for the allied armies; attaining in 1918 a daily output of one and a half million pounds of guncotton, it was the wonder city of the world war. The Hopewell Plant, built near Petersburg, Virginia, on a famous Civil War battle ground, is a monument to American organization and patriotism.

At the start of the war, barren; quiet haven for generations; cherishing the memories of the heroes of the North and South. Within a year, an industrial behemoth, hustling, bustling and producing: surrounded by a city of 40,000 happy souls, with handsome homes, cozy cottages, hotels, clubs, schools, stores, churches and theatres, improved streets, electric lights, plumbing, sewers, lawns, gardens, fire and police protection, trolleys, ice plants and all the conveniences that modern municipal engineering has devised.

That is Hopewell as it stood on that memorable November 11, 1918. Then industry stopped. But not for long. Hopewell is young, vigorous and whole. It stands today the embodiment of latent powers and opportunity. Already it is feeling the magic touch of new industry and is springing again into magnificent action-to do its great part in the reconstruction of a world its former product helped to devastate.

At the writing (Sept. 1, 1920) eleven new industries are operating or preparing to operated at Hopewell. To all corners of the globe Hopewell products will soon go forth in the shape of Trunks and Bags, Steel Tools, Electric Insulation, Cotton and Wool Waste, Paper Pulp, High-Grade China, Artificial Silk Paper Board and various other commodities.

Hopewell is a selective, diversified industrial community, and only those industries which are not detrimental and which themselves can benefit by locating at Hopewell are invited to become members of Hopewell's industrial family. No other community can show so many new industries, can show so many new industries attracted in so short a time and attracted without the sweet-sounding inducements so often held out as "bait" for the industrial home-seeker. Hopewell's advantages are real—both natural and created. In reproductions from recent photographs, they are presented for you consideration in the following pages.

DU POINT CHEMICAL COMPANY
INCORPORATED
WILMINGTON, DELAWARE

AERIAL VIEW OF CELANESE CORPORATION OF AMERICA PLANT

Mrs. Pace's son and daughter in law; Thompson Gardenhire Pace Jr. &
Christine (Tina) Staples Pace 26 years Old

Patricia Louise Rose Pace with 1st Grandson,
Thompson Gardenhire Pace, III

One of Sue Pace's closest & dearest friends, Becky Rackley Putney

1941– Martha Sue Pace's 21st Birthday in City Point Hopewell

1941 - Letter written by my grandfather, and grandmother, Thompson G. Pace, Sr., and Patricia Louise Pace to their daughter, my Mother, Martha Sue Pace.

"Your Birthday"

Friday the 13th is my lucky day, and as they put you in my arms I heard your daddy say. "Her mouth is like a rosebud, her eyes are heavenly blue– so we will give her our Mother's name and call her "Martha Sue."

You have been all that we have wished for twenty one short years– and not once have you given us cause, to shed a tear. Our hopes for you my darling, has been a world of love. And wishes for much happiness like the happiness you've given us.

Mother & Daddy

"Merry Xmas"

Dear —

Just could not find
a "Card that says
"I love you"

My wish for you sweet
is health and happiness
and all the joys it
can bring, Not only
for this Xmas but Many.
Many more and every
day between —

May 1943 bring peace
throughout the World
and the light shine
more bright for each one.

Mother

Thomas Gardenhire Pace Sr.
Dies In Hospital—1947

Well Known Hopewell Citizen Passes In Richmond—
Rites Tomorrow

(Hopewell Bureau)

Thomas G. Pace, 59, of 208 Ramsey Avenue, well known citizen of Hopewell since 1915, died Wednesday afternoon in a Richmond hospital

During the past several years he has held a responsible position with the DuPont—Hercules Company, which operates a large chemical plant at Hopewell.

During the years of his residence in his adopted home town, Tom Pace had become one of its leading substantial citizens as was evidenced by the large number of citizens who were present when the last sad rites were spoken over his remains; and the profusion of floral offerings which were contributed by his friends in loving tribute to his memory.

A native of Trenton, Ga. He has been active in civic and fraternal circles, being a past chancellor commander of Hopewell Lodge 141, Knights of Pythians, Roanoke Chapter of the DOKKIES, active member of Hopewell Aerie, Fraternal Order of Eagles, and of First Methodist Church. For the past 27 years he has been employed in the local silk plant.

He is survived by his wife: Mrs. Patricia Louise Pace daughter Miss Martha Sue Pace, of Hopewell, so Thomas G. Pace, Jr., of Petersburg and a grandson, Thomas G. Pace, III, of Petersburg; two sisters: Mrs. Ethel McCorkle, of Thomason, Ga., Mrs. Holmes Morrow, of Tussville, Ala., and one brother, Jerry C. Pace, of Trenton, Ga.

Funeral services will be held in the chapel of the Hopewell Funeral Parlors at 4 o'clock Friday afternoon.

The Rev. R. W. Vanderberry, pastor of First Methodist Church, will officiate. Interment will be in Sunset Memorial Park, Chester.

Thomas G. Pace—Dies in Virginia; *by C.S. Turner*

While convalescing from a minor operation in a Richmond hospital, Thomas G. Pace, a former citizen of Dade county, died unexpectedly on April 3rd. His attending physician attributed his sudden death to a blood clot having reached his heart from the surgical operation performed a few days before.

Thomas Gardenhire Pace was born and reared in Trenton, the son of the late Jeremiah Gardenhire (shook) Pace and Mrs. Susan Gardenhire Pace, member of a prominent pioneer family.

While yet a young man, some 20 or 30 years ago, the deceased left his home county and located at Hopewell, Va., where he married and reared his family.

During the past several years he has held a responsible position with the Du Pont-Hercules Company, which operates a large chemical plant at Hopewell.

Thomas Pace leaves to survive his passing, his wife; one son, T.G. Pace Jr., one daughter, Miss Susan Pace, brother Jerry C. Pace, and all of Hopewell; two sisters, Mrs. Ethel McCorkle, of Thorason, Ga., and Mrs. Homer E. Morrow of Trussville, Ala.

Remains of the deceased were interred in the beautiful Hopewell cemetery. The citizens of Trenton and Dade county all deeply sympathize with the family in their bereavement.

AUTHOR'S NOTES:

A paradigm of education and family excellence:

Grandmother helped parents understand that she created a sacred holy space. When children came over the threshold of Mrs. Pace's school, they were in a place where they were cherished. They were in an education workplace where they were challenged, treasured, and in a place of change. Grandmother was a talented and gifted optimist with a strong educational vision. She was a driven dreamer.

There are significant moments in everyone's life that deserve to be captured. Mrs. Pace's Kindergarten story is passionate enough to be preserved in a book. This was a family education business where emotions, personalities and dramatic plays shined through – creating memories that last a lifetime. Every picture tells a story.

Mrs. Pace with 1st grandson, Thompson G. Pace III

Chapter 1: A Vision

The annual graduation ceremony was a professionally scripted and directed production complete with costumes and printed playbills. The musical plays provided a part for every child enrolled in the school! These included, The Magic Carpet, Working on the Railroad, Cowboy Roundup, The Balloon Man, and other productions whose records survive in the collection of programs that has been maintained by the family for over 75 years. One can just imagine the delight of the parents, relatives and friends when they watched their little ones singing "Take Off Your Troubles and Put on a Smile" or "If I knew You Were Coming, I'd Have Baked a Cake." Mrs. Pace made it easy on the families— all costumes were provided by the School—she sewed them herself! The productions were community-inspired efforts because the school partnered with the Christmas plays and spring concerts performed in the lovely Art Deco auditorium of Patrick Copeland School in Downtown Hopewell.

Mrs. Pace's school evokes a time when "neighborhood" had a special meaning – she walked to work, less than two house lengths away but across the railroad bridge in City Point. She quite often led the children, organized and holding hands, to her house for playtime in her garden. When the children "graduated" they could walk to their neighborhood elementary school. Long-time teachers at Mrs. Pace's included, Mrs. Pace, Mrs. Laura Woehr, Mrs. Mary Agnes Merner, Mrs. Virginia (Diddy) Ford Flannagan, and Mrs. Martha Sue Pace Traylor who took over operations after her mother's death in 1961.

The Pace/Traylor Family exhibited the best of Hopewell—an entrepreneurial family, offering their valued and professional services to the community in a manner that leaves those associated with them with many fond memories of Hopewell.

Having been reared in this environment, it was many years before I realized what I had. T. S. Eliot expresses so beautifully my own perception and conviction: "We must not cease from exploration. And the end of all our exploring will be to arrive where we began and to know the place for the first time."

Mrs. Pace's Kindergarten spanned forty-five years in the life of a young business woman before and during the Children's Day Care Revolution in America.

During that time, many people struggled to build a children's education utopia based on the unique ideals in a curriculum of studies, arts and drama. Mrs. Pace's Kindergarten ranked as one of the best of these efforts.

This book provides Mrs. Pace's journey through life before she reached the family happiness backdrop at last. She was a girl of quiet strength and startling beauty, released into the fascinating world of Hopewell nobility, a widow at fifty-seven with a young daughter, Martha Sue Pace Traylor, and brother Thompson G. Pace Jr. As a single mother, she had little money and few prospects during the war years. Determined and inquisitive, she survived, maintaining her humanity and sense of decency, and created a breathtakingly inventive education center. Keeping her eye fixed on her first love, children, she ascended from obscurity to one of the most passionate architects of the Children's Day Care industry beginning in 1941.

Patricia Louise Ross Pace

*(the following article was printed in the Hopewell News
1961 while Mrs. Pace was still living)*

Woman of the Week
By Dorothy Moore

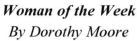

*"Working with people and children is wonderful," according to Mrs. T. G. Pace. She
shares the happy life and the sad life of parents by helping take care of their children.*

*From babysitting to full-time kindergarten work, Mrs. Pace has given a lot of her time and
talent to entertaining youngsters.*

*Born Patricia Louise Ross in New London, N.C., Mrs. Pace was the daughter of the late
Mr. & Mrs. R. J. Ross. Young Patty grew up in New London and later graduated from Lenoir Rhyne College in Hickory, N.C. 1909 where she studied business.*

*Miss Ross was a buyer and bookkeeper for about three years in a retail business operated by
her father and brother. Later she spent several months touring California and Texas with
friends.*

Marriage

Miss Ross and Thompson G. Pace Sr. married in 1915 and came to Hopewell where he was employed by the Tubize Company. Mrs. Pace has watched the town grow from a few buildings to a modern city.

Two children were born to the couple: Thompson Pace, Jr. who now lives in Colonial Heights, and their daughter, Mrs. William E. Traylor, who makes her home with her mother at 206 Ramsey Avenue. Both of Mrs. Pace's children have young sons, and she delights in telling them stories and entertaining them.

It was during World War II that Mrs. Pace's keen interest in children began. The great number of army wives who were transferred to Camp Lee would many times be without a baby sitter in times of need, and Mrs. Pace would ask them to let her keep the children.

One summer Mrs. Pace kept her enclosed back yard available for babies and children to stay in when their mothers were shopping or away on business. The numbers increased so rapidly that Mrs. Pace was obliged to hire two young girls to help her with them.

As the weather began to get cooler, her problems increased, so she set up a day nursery in her home. After her husband's death in 1947, she continued her nursery and the following year decided to open a kindergarten and nursery school at the Brown Apartments.

There are two large rooms for children from three to six years old in the nursery and kindergarten.

35

"Sunken Streets"
(photo: DuPont Scrapbook, Appomattox Regional Library)

Back Yard Play

Mrs. Pace is a member of the First Methodist Church.

She says that she still corresponds with a number of the former service people who lived here during the war. She has kept children from nearly every state in the union, from Cuba, England, France and Germany. Some of the children were not able to speak English when she took them, but as she says, "children are not hard to understand."

Patient, kindhearted and generous, Mrs. Pace has been the Good Samaritan to many transients and to townspeople as well."

———————— *end of Moore article* ————————

39

Mrs. Pace's School started in her home at
208 Ramsey Avenue Hopewell, VA. Today's view of home.

Early pictures of home-school with Mrs. Pace's daughter-Mother—1941

MRS. THOMAS PACE
PLAY DAY NURSERY

208 RAMSEY AVENUE
CITY POINT

CHILDREN 2 YEARS AND OLDER _____ 10c per Hr.
CHILDREN UNDER 2 YEARS _____ 20c per Hr.
CHILDREN BY DAY _____ 75c
MEALS _____ 25c

(For Mothers Who Work)

SPECIAL RATES PER WEEK
VACATION RATES

Phone 2846

MRS. PACE'S KINDERGARTEN
AND NURSERY SCHOOL

RHYTHM BAND, DANCING, SPATTER PAINTING
CREATIVE ART, PROGRESSIVE PRE SCHOOL TRAINING
TRAINED SUPERVISION

BROWN APT.
CITY POINT

OPPOSITE
CITY POINT INN

Mrs. Pace's business cards: 1941 at 208 Ramsey Avenue City Point & 1949 Licensed Brown Apartments City Point Hopewell, Virginia

43

MRS. PACE'S KINDERGARTEN DOCTRINE

Mrs. Pace's Kindergarten became a Hopewell tradition for forty-five years.

One of my favorite education mentors was Fred Rogers, who recently left this world. I think he said best how I feel about my grandmother, Mrs. Patricia Louise Ross Pace.

There was a moment, at the 1998 Daytime Emmys when Mr. Rogers was presented with a Lifetime Achievement Award. Mr. Rogers went onstage to accept the award and there, in front of all the soap opera stars and talk show synchrotrons, in front of all the jutting man-tanned jaws and jutting saltwater bosoms, he made his small bow and said into the microphone: "All of us have special ones who have loved us into being. Would you just take, along with me, ten seconds to think of the people who have helped you become who you are?" And then he lifted his wrist, looked at the audience, looked at his watch, and said; "I'll watch the time."

There was at first, a small whoop from the crowd, a giddy, strangled hiccup of laughter, as people realized that he wasn't kidding, that Mister Rogers was not some convenient eunuch, but rather a man, an authority figure who actually expected them to do what he asked. And so they did. One second, two seconds, three seconds -- and now the jaws clenched, and the bosoms heaved, and the mascara ran, and the tears fell upon the glittered gathering like rain leaking down a crystal chandelier. And Mister Rogers finally looked up from his watch and said softly, "May God be with you and to all his vanquished children."

Daycare began to emerge during the 1940's as an educational, beneficial experience for children of various social classes whose mothers and fathers both worked outside the home, and a public service for which the government might take responsibility. This new definition stood uneasily next to, and often clashed with, the older understanding of daycare as a private charitable enterprise, offering custodial care under less-than-ideal circumstances for the children of poor families disrupted by a mother's need to go out to work.

This was common with other sections of the country. There were many well-meaning efforts by young women of leisure and small means, combining a fondness for children and a desire to augment income, opening a so-called kindergarten and nursery. Mrs. Pace first called hers just, "Mrs. Pace's."

Throughout the time period covered in this book, Mrs. Pace's Kindergarten daycare was transformed from a charity for desperate single mothers to a widespread need of many families, and a legitimate public asset. From its origin as an elite women's effort, Mrs. Pace's school brought neglected children off the streets and her daycare became a way for ordinary families to get help raising their children. These children were blessed by an experience that stressed socialization and building imagination.

Group child care during the late 1940s and 1950s remained unpopular. Eventually, however, daycare gained further acceptance due to the growing realization that day had potential to be educational and thus to benefit children.

Daycare Becomes "Educational"

A crucial aspect of the growing legitimacy of daycare was the conviction that day-care was educational and thus benefited children. The connection between the wartime day care centers and the public schools had helped strengthen the connection between day care and education.

The real children's education goal remains to this day a controversial environment. Mrs. Pace's school provided education to future physicians, lawyers, judges, teacher's and many prominent business owners of the Hopewell Community. She was a woman of resolute purpose, who presided over many educational trials, often resulting in great accomplishments, until passing. Her efforts changed the lives of her students, fostering a moral sense and love of community and nation.

Head Start...generated positive feelings about day care's potential to improve children's lives. Created in 1965 as part of the War on Poverty...Its goals combined those of the charitable day nursery with those of the nursery school. Head Start's popularity helped legitimize the idea of educationally oriented day care for all children.

The second World War and economic crisis not only forced families to send mothers into the workplace, but it also prompted charitable day nurseries and the federal government to revise their attitudes toward day care, albeit temporarily.

Private day nurseries expanded their scope (not only for children of working mothers, but for any child whose family was experiencing hardship). The federal government sponsored public nursery schools throughout the country.

However, day care was excluded from the welfare system established by the Social Security Act of 1935 and its subsequent amendments, as... "Mothers' pensions had already gained recognition as the social policy of choice for poor women and children, overshadowing day care...(and) was written into federal law." (SS Act)

My professional pursuits led me to explore the origins of the education system and its parallels to American jurisprudence in working for the State Department of Education for twenty-one years.

I was educated in North Carolina as was my grandmother, who attended Lenoir Ryan College. I have spent many years as a practicing educator and nurse in Hopewell, Virginia.

My research took me into the archives of Hopewell's City Point community. I discovered that Hopewell's success and growth resonates deeply within my affection for history and narrative. This story emerged unbidden, prompted by a dear close friend and teacher, Joyce Pritchard, and the fact that I spent my childhood growing up in this wonderful education environment.

By 1950 to the 1970's, working mothers were no longer objects of pity, but simply members of society whose needs had to be addressed. Daycare was thus no longer just a gift bestowed on the poor by benevolent philanthropists, but a service that mothers and child welfare advocates insisted the government had an obligation to provide. Mrs. Pace's day care programs themselves were no longer seen as daytime orphanages, but as a type of school, providing enriching experiences that would nurture children's emotions. She had a concept and vision long before our government felt an obligation to provide education for preschoolers.

"1942-Federal Government passes the Lanham Act, providing federal funding for child care across the country as part of the war effort because women were needed in the workforce."

The City Point area of Hopewell where Mrs. Pace started her school, is historic as one of the oldest continually occupied English settlements in the United States. During the Civil War, City Point served as headquarters for Ulysses S. Grant, during the siege of nearby Petersburg. Many historic buildings and sites remain in Hopewell.

Grandmother was one who never accepted the facts. When you are really good, there are no facts. There are just children's lives to save that have been placed in your hands. To all who read my family business history book, education is the greatest work that anyone can do. It is this work that creates the future of man.

Grandmother's education environment was so special to Hopewell's community that phone calls continue to this day asking for possible enrollment.

From 1941 through 1986, the Pace/Traylor Family of City Point cared for thousands of Hopewell children at their family-owned Hopewell School of Childhood, first known simply as "Mrs. Pace's." This was not just "babysitting." From its very beginning, this institution provided to Hopewell families a priceless creative environment, first offered to Hopewell children for only ten cents per hour.

This book is to honor these two great educators, grandmother, Mrs. Pace and her daughter, mother, Martha Sue Pace Traylor and their school, "Mrs. Pace's Kindergarten & Nursery and The Hopewell School of Childhood." Their powerful pilot school was licensed in 1948 as Hopewell's First Children's Education center.

The day-care license is issued and monitored by The Commonwealth of Virginia Department of Social Services Licensing Division.

Licensed programs must meet the standards promulgated by the Child Day-Care Council. The Virginia Department of Social Services enforces these standards by inspecting centers at least twice a year and investigating complaints.

Many foreign immigrants flocked to Hopewell during the World War II boom. Many came from (Camp Lee) Ft. Lee Army Base. They often spoke little or no English and therefore depended on manual labor as a source of income. Greeks, Italians, Syrians, Russians, Armenians, Lebanese, Turks, Jews, and Slovaks could all be found in large numbers within the Hopewell city limits. Mrs. Pace believed that "a good teacher can reach anyone," as she mentioned in many Hopewell News articles. Teachers like grandmother made all the difference. She welcomed one and all to a different learning center environment.

HOPEWELL SCHOOL of CHILDHOOD
PACE'S
KINDERGARTEN and NURSERY SCHOOL
HOPEWELL - VIRGINIA
19___ to -19___

PUPILS NAME _____

TEACHER _Sue Pace Traylor_

DIRECTOR _Lannie Pace_

I show an interest in books and pictures

I work and play well with others

I tell stories well

I take part in dramatic play

I can color, paint, cut and work with craft materials

I take part in singing and music

EXPLANATION OF MARKS

O - Outstanding
S - Satisfactory
N - Needs to improve

I skip, hop and march in time	I listen when others are speaking

I do my memory work well	I do my Pre-school work, (numbers, letters, etc.)

HiSTory Bible Geography Language Science Astronomy

I am always clean and neat	I use a clean handerchief or tissue

Days Attended _____

Days Absent _____

Tends to use correct English											
Keeps hands off others											
Responds well in rhythm band											
Responds to suggestions											
Takes off and puts on own wraps											
Respects property of others											
Shows ability in leadership											

Weight									
Height									

Parents signature

1950

Laura Dickinson Woehr, Mrs. Pace's First Kindergarten Teacher

Laura Dickinson Woehr was born May 20, 1915 on a farm in Oswego County, New York. She attended a one-room school house during grade school. Her high school years were spent at Baldwinsville Academy a few miles away form her home. She was the valedictorian of her class.

After graduation, Laura went to Oswego Normal school where she received her teaching certificate. She also met her future husband, Frederick Woehr, who was pursuing a degree in Industrial Arts Education. She returned to a one-room schoolhouse in her rural community for two years, but this time as a teacher.

Laura and Frederick were married in 1937 and they moved to Hopewell, Virginia where he had secured a job as the Industrial Arts teacher for Hopewell High School. They had two children, Anne and Fred, Jr. When Fred was four years old, Laura Woehr began teaching at Mrs. Pace's Kindergarten in City Point. She taught there for five years before becoming a teacher for Hopewell City Schools. Both Laura and Frederick Woehr retired after many years of dedicated service to students in Hopewell.

9:00 - 9:25 A.M. — Supervised Free Play

9:25 - 9:30   — Put Things Away

9:30 - 9:45   — Good Morning Songs, Morning Prayer, Roll Call, Counting Health Inspection.

9:45 - 10:00   — Conversation about various topics. or Poems or Finger Play or Work book

10:05 - 10:15   — Music (Songs, Rhythms)
                      or
                    Listening to Records
                      or
                    Clay Modeling
                      or
                    Creative Art Work

10:15 - 10:30   — Wash hands, grace, lunch

10:30 - 11:00   — Rest - Heads on Table

11:00 - 11:20   — Rhythm Band or Dancing

11:20 - 11:45   — Playground, if nice

11:45 - 11:55   — Story Time - Dramatization

12:00   — Dismissal

Chapter 3: Growing Together

My family were pioneers in combining daycare with varied education. I celebrate their leadership and vision through dramatic acts of vision.

To grow up and be educated in grandmother's learning center environment, was to be gifted beyond expectations. I might say forthrightly, in writing this book, that I never do anything without prayer. I could not have become the successful person I am today without asking God's help, to make it right. Perhaps something I say will make a difference in a child's life.

Like any successful daycare business, Mrs. Pace's kindergarten did more than just warehouse children. It also reinforced family values in her home, 208 Ramsey Avenue, City Point Virginia where she created an angelic environment by climbing the ladder to success and taking her family with her.

Mrs. Pace's had a social paradigm as an education center. The word "paradigm" comes from the Greek. For our purposes, a simple way to understand paradigms is to see them as maps. We all know that "the map is not the territory." A map is simply an explanation of certain aspects of the territory. That's exactly what a paradigm is - a theory, an explanation, or model of a greater reality. You can't have the fruits without the roots.

My pioneering family history illustrates grandmother's teaching inspirations. She and my grandfather were educators and entrepreneurs. My grandfather was intuitive and my grandmother was creative and reasoning. These qualities when balanced drove their business venture to success.

In a time when many people were off to war and struggling for jobs I am sure the coming education age was pretty frightening. Grandmother, as I was told by mother, prepared children not only to compete, but also to thrive in Hopewell city and community. This was no small task.

It was not enough for her to teach them just to read and write, to add a column of numbers or recite facts and figures. Mrs. Pace's children were also taught to think, to be analytical, and to be dramatic, artistic and creative. Her theories, philosophy and methodology in education therefore included dance, music, theatre, and the visual arts.

Mother always told me that grandmother taught her teachers that what you believe in can never be a secret to the children, because everything you do reveals what it is you really believe. It doesn't matter what you say, really, because children can read your behavior.

Mrs. Pace started teaching in her home at 206 Ramsey Avenue in 1941 along with Mrs. Laura Dickinson Woehr, who was grandmother's first Kindergarten teacher. When the school became licensed in 1948 it moved to the lower floor of Brown Apartments on East Broadway, opposite the City Point Inn. Children were educated and taken care of for ten cents an hour. The school relocated and moved in 1958 to the newly built school, 519 Appomattox Street. This was a new home for Mrs. Pace, her daughter, son-in-law and children. Now the school is my beloved home; yes, that's right, I live in the school house.

Mrs. Pace's teaching lessons were designed to make sure other people's highest priority needs for their children were being met. Many former teachers revealed to me that they learned more from Mrs. Pace and mother than they ever did in their college studies.

Mrs. Pace's son, Thompson Gardinhire Pace, Jr. with children,
at 208 Ramsey Avenue Hopewell

1947- Mr. William E. Traylor Sr. dating Mrs. Pace's daughter, Martha Sue Pace at Mrs. Pace's School in the Brown Apartments

A helper with Mrs. Pace's daughter-in-law, Christine Staples Pace

January 1, 1948— Licensed Day Care

New School Starts Here

Nursery And Kindergarten To Open January 2 In Brown Apartments

(Hopewell Bureau)

A nursery school and kindergarden, operated by Mrs. Thomas Pace, will open Monday in the Brown Apartments.

Registration will be held tomorrow from 2 to 5 p. m. Parents will be given an opportunity to view the school and its modern equipment.

Two rooms are being utilized for the school. A nursery will be held in one portion of the building while the other portion is to be used for the kindergarden. A partition will divide the two sections of the school and qualified teachers will be assigned to each of the departments.

Equipment in the two departments is most modern and of sturdy construction. Many new innovations for the entertainment and interest of the children are being introduced.

Mrs. Pace is well known in Hopewell. She has conducted a nursery in her home for several years and because of the many requests and the limited space, she has expanded the program and moved the school to the Brown Apartments.

New School Starts Here: 1948

Nursery and Kindergarten To Open January 2nd In Brown Apartments

(Hopewell Bureau)

A nursery school and kindergarten, operated by Mrs. Thomas Pace, will open Monday in the Brown Apartments.

Registration will be held tomorrow from 2 to 5 p. m. Parents will be given an opportunity to view the school and its modern equipment.

Two rooms are being utilized for the school. A nursery will be held in one portion of the building while the other portion is to be used for the kindergarten. A partition will divide the two sections of the school and qualified teachers will be assigned to each of the departments.

Equipment in the two departments is mostly modern and of sturdy construction. Many new innovations for the entertainment and interest of the children are being introduced.

Mrs. Pace is well known in Hopewell. She has conducted a nursery in her home for several years, and because of the many requests and the limited space, she has expanded the program and moved the school to the Brown Apartments.

_____*End of Hopewell News Article*_____

One of my first impressions of grandmother, told by mother, was that she did not believe in differentiating between students based on their past, their skills, or their ethnicity. She believed that tracking a child based on an impression risk prevented that child from reaching his or her potential. She saw her task as one of nurturing potential and encouraging achievement, even if the greater Hopewell community saw no such potential in some of her students

This approach to education that I saw modeled by my grandmother, my mother, and my father, is engraved upon my heart. I became a teacher not to judge, but to empower. Grandmother helped parents to understand that she was creating a <u>sacred holy space.</u> Her school was the antithesis of what some people expected, particularly in their children, who were labeled disadvantaged, at risk, or poor. Her children could not control the home they came from.

To help solve this poverty situation in Hopewell, she used community collaboration. In her time, leaders from the community agreed to work collaboratively with grandmother to provide comprehensive community based educational services for Hopewell's children. Their bold action recognized that home-grown education solutions would enhance long-term productivity within the Hopewell population, and generate additional revenue by keeping money for service in the city. It was family, community and school working together. Her students gave back to the Hopewell community before they ever left.

Many honored Hopewell businesses are run by students who learned to rebuild and strengthen, by visiting the community schools, banks, legal offices, real-estate offices, police station, fire department and the nursing homes, as the pictures in this book show. They were exposed to all different types of careers and encouraged to pursue livelihoods, to explore or question, to perceive relationships between fields of knowledge and experiences. Grandmother explored different kinds of education with no oppression. By discovering and building on each child's strengths, she instilled a lifetime of enthusiasm for learning

Every teacher in Mrs. Pace's school was aware of her responsibility to create her sacred space. When a child came through the door of her school they were in a place where they were cherished, challenged, treasured, and in a place of change.

I'm convinced that too often parents are also trapped in the management paradigm, thinking of control, efficiency, and rules instead of direction, purpose, and feelings of family.

Education in and among families, friends, neighbors and even people in the community, gave children so much.

Past teachers working for Mrs. Pace's School during the years said that it was the most rewarding position they ever had, although it was the most challenging. When you walked through Mrs. Pace's doors, it was one fascination after another. It would drain a lot out of you, but what her children gave were what I call "lessons of love," because they were family. She shaped tough family education to help create the children's own identities. Family is the main engine of education. The curriculum of family is at the heart of any good life.

If you treat employees as if they make a difference to the company, they will make a difference. That's been the employee-focused philosophy behind my family's business beliefs since my grandmother opened Hopewell's first children's daycare center in 1941. At the heart of this unique paradigm business is a simple idea: satisfied employees create satisfied customers.

What did it take to make this great school? It took committed teaching leaders like my grandmother and mother; employed teachers like; Mrs. Frederick Laura Woehr, Mrs. Mary Agnes Merner, Mrs. Carol Flack, Mrs. Virginia (Diddy) Flannagan, Mrs. Sally Carwile, Mrs. Edwina Moore Daniel, Mrs. Donna Myers, Mrs. Patricia Frederickson, Mrs. Theda Lee, Mrs. Ellen Garvin, and Miss Faith Farris.

Education standards dictate that no school is a great school if children are not achieving. It's not just about teaching children to read and write. It's about teaching them to think, love, be artistic, speak well, behave in society in exceptional ways, to be economically independent and be able to contribute back to society.

Grandmother's school teaching methodology was unique and different, focused on student achievement and making the ordinary child extraordinary. One former student who attended during the fifties told me, "in Mrs. Pace's house she used to wear a farmer's hat and would kill a chicken by wringing it's neck." She also said, "that was the only painful experience she ever had there." She remembered "health inspections telling each child to hold out their hands to see how clean they were."

Grandmother's theory was that, if the kids in her school were not learning, the teachers were doing something wrong, not the students. Nowhere in that description is there anything about economic income level.

She was an innovative futurist who excited students about learning. As a result, she passed along a gift much more powerful than knowledge: the skills for a lifetime of learning.

Early childhood education can determine how children feel about learning for the rest of their lives. Many teachers stress discipline and conformity as the key to educating young children, I am certain that grandmother taught freedom, individuality, creativity and imagination, which may be an even more valuable lesson.

SANTA VISITS NURSERY—The picture above was made Christmas Eve at Mrs. Pace's Nursery School when children were given presents by Santa Claus. Those in the picture are: standing (left to right) Mary Bartha, Terry Streetman, Bobby Lakins, Madison Aderholt, Carolyn Dolsey, Bill Elliot, David England, Margrete Kelly, Judy Elliot, Kuyka, Aderhole, Carolyn Petree and Andra England; sitting, George Ameen, Mary Lewis Thomas, Sharon Lee Hensley, Hugh Douglas, Darnel Force, Carolyn Dolsey and Carlo Milton. Those not in the picture because of absence on account of illness are Connie Douglas and Elizabeth Broaddus, Janie Frampton and Becky Lou Richardson were out of the city. (Scott Photo).

January 4, 1948 at Mrs. Paces home and Nursery school.

Standing (left to right): Mary Bartha, Terry Streetman, Bobby Lakins, Madison Aderholt, Carolyn Dolsey, Bill Elliott, David England, Margrette Kelly, Judy Elliott, Kuyka Aderholt, Carolyn Petree, Andra England; sitting: George Ameen, Mary Lewis Thomas, Sharon Lee Hensley, Hugh Douglas, Darnel Force, Carolyn Dolsey and Carlo Milton. Those not in the picture because of absence on account of illness are Connie Douglas and Elizabeth Broaddus. Janie Frampton and Becky Lou Richardson were out of the city. (Scott Photo).

One from many of Mrs. Pace's students to become a teacher, Connie Douglas was born on May 11, 1941 in Hopewell and was a lifelong resident of the city. She graduated from Hopewell High School in 1959, earned a Bachelor of Science degree in Business Administration from the University of Richmond in 1962, and earned a Master of Education degree from Virginia State University in 1988.

Connie was an elementary school teacher for her entire professional career, a veteran of forty-one years in the Hopewell and Prince George County public school systems. She concentrated on reading education, teaching Title 1 Reading Recovery, and was named the Richmond Area Reading Council, Reading Teacher of the Year. She served the schools in a variety of other capacities, including work on school accreditation committees and as a Grad Level Chairman. She was twice the recipient of service awards from the Hopewell School Board. Outside of teaching, her passions later in life included work with the Woman's Club of Hopewell, the John Randolph Foundation, the Historic Hopewell Foundation and others. At other times, she was active in volunteer activities related to her children, including work with the Cub Scouts and Hopewell High School Band. She loved to play the piano and was a active member of the First United Methodist Church in Hopewell.

August 13, 1949 Wedding—Martha Sue Pace Traylor and
Mother of the Bride, Mrs. Patricia Louise Pace

Pace's Kindergarten
Opens September 8, 1949
(Hopewell News)

Mrs. Pace's Kindergarten and Nursery School will open September 8 in the Brown Apartments City Point.

On Friday, September 4 from 9 until 12 noon parents are urged to bring their children to visit the school rooms and enroll their children in the school.

Mrs. Pace, in announcing the opening, stated that everything for the children's enjoyment will be found at the school including the rhythm band, spatter painting, finger painting, etc. Some pre-school work is taught in the Kindergarten section with Mrs. Frederick Woehr as teacher. A well equipped enclosed play yard is in use each day the weather permits.

Youthful members of the Mrs. Pace's Kindergarten, "Hopewell School Of Childhood," are shown above. They are, first row left to right: David Bitton, Harry Heckle, Peter Furbush, Terry Streetman, Nat Daily, Billy Graham, Tommy Lakin; second row: Ronald Hickenbury, Brady Rackley, Mechelle Coxon, Dianne Forbes, Mary Bartha, Freddy Woehr; third row: Frances Willard, Kathleen Anderson, Judy Jones, Jeff Willard, Lynn Erdman, Nancy Croom, and Carla Melton. Not present when the picture was taken were: Suzy Smith, Robin Jenks, Jimmy Kestner, and Michael Pritchard.

1950 *Youthful members of Mrs. Pace's Kindergarten, "Hopewell School of Childhood,"*
They are first row left to right: David Bitton, Harry Heckle, Peter Furbush, Terry Streetman,
Nat Daily, Billy Graham, Tommy Lakin; second row: Ronald Hickenbury, Brady Rackley,
Mechelle Coxon, Diane Forbes, Mary Bartha, Freddy Woehr; third row: Frances Willard,
Kathleen Anderson, Judy Jones, Jeff Willard Lynn Erdman, Nancy Croom, and Carla Mel-
ton. Not present when the picture was taken were: Suzy Smith, Robin Jenks, Jimmy Kestner,
and Michael Pritchard.

1950 Program Closes

The first annual commencement of Pace's School Kindergarten
Presents Entertainment At End of Session (Hopewell News)

Closing exercise and awarding of Diplomas to children in Mrs. Pace's Kindergar-
ten were held Friday morning in the Kindergarten room in Brown Apartments, Broadway
and Allen Ave.

Mrs. Frederick Woehr, teacher, presented the program. Jeff Willard welcomed the
group with the good morning song and the morning prayer was given by the class, Freddy
Woehr was the announcer.

The class sang a group of songs with motion following a dance that was presented
by Corla Melton, Nancy Groom and Mary Bertha.

Billy Graham recited the poem. "The Kitten" while the poem "The Stars' was given by Ronnie Hockenbury. Kathleen Anderson recited "A Little Seed" and Francis Willard read the poem, "A Bird With A Yellow Bill." Lynn Erman recited "Signs of Spring."

An interpretive dance was presented by Lynn Erdman, Michelle Coxon, Kathleen Anderson, and Diane Forbes.

"We are Little Indians" dance was given by Freddy Woehr, David Button, Peter Furbush, Harry Heckler, Tommy Lakin, Ronnie Hockenbury, Jeff Willard, Nat Dailey and Larry Streitman."

"Rocka By Baby" was given by Nancy Croom, Dianne Forbes, Lynn Erdman, Michelle Coxon, Judy Jones, Kathleen Anderson, Francis Willard, and Mary Elizabeth Bertha.

A folk dance, "Skip To My Lou" was presented by the entire class. Those receiving diplomas were: Brady Lee Rackley, Frederick Woehr. Peter Furbush, Terry Streetman, Jeff Willard, Ronnie Hocklenbury, Judy Jones, Nancy Croom, Robin Jenks, Dianne Forbes, Kathleen Anderson, Lynn Erdman, and Mary Elizabeth Bartha.

Prizes were awarded to Mary Elizabeth Bartha and Freddy Woehr, for having a perfect attendance since January 1. Judy Jones closed the program.

———————————*End of Hopewell News Article*———————————

Today, Freddy Woehr Royster, grandson of Laura Woehr, is now the Principal of Hopewell's Carter G. Woodson School.

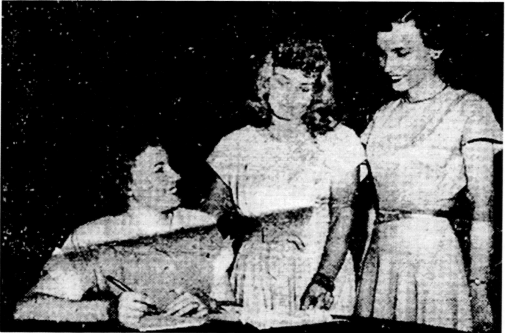

Among the members of Beta Mu Sorority which held its first convention of Richmond since before the War, are Sue Pace, Registrar of Hopewell; Margaret Nicholas of Petersburg, and Dena Loper of Colonial Heights.

NATIONAL PRESIDENT—Mrs. Sue Pace Traylor to the national presidency of Beta Mu Sorority, is shown above. She is a resident of Hopewell and has been active in both Omicron Chapter in Hopewell and the Gamma Province.

*March 8, 1951—The **RYTHYM BAND** from Mrs. Pace's Kindergarten is shown above when they played several numbers at the Beta Mu Fashion Show recently. The director is Bill Graham, from left to right the band members in the first row: are Carol Stewart, Bettye Kirby, and Mary Bartha, Second row: Bendie Holt, Carol Heckle, Billy Belk, David Jones, Jimmie Halpin, and Gibby Button. Third row: Walter Sheally, Harry Heckle, Jerry Yoaklm, Margaret Perry, Elisa Turner, Joe Shambough. Forth row: Nancy Gillespie, Sandra Walker, Michael Prichard, Johnny Perry, Dorothy Grainger, Al Glass, Terry Jenks, and Steve Koledoke*

Beta Mu Fashion Show Attracts Large Audience
Local models showed new spring fashions to a large audience at he Beta Mu Fashion Show
last Friday night in the Hopewell High School Auditorium.
H. M. "Buzz" Ford. Jr., as master of ceremonies helped to make the show sponsored by
Omicron Chapter of Beta Mu Sorority very successful.

On the program were Mrs. Pace's Kindergarten Rhythm Band, three-year- old Janet Amoon
and Miss Jackie Morris who danced and singer James C. Morris.

1952—Surrounded by many young admirers Santa Claus when he visited Mrs. Pace's Nursery and Kindergarten on Friday afternoon. The Christmas party marked the closing of the school until January. (Alvin Jones Studio)

Mrs. Pace's Nursery-Kindergarten Closed With Christmas Festivities 1952

(Hopewell News)

A Christmas party complete with carol singing, gifts, and Santa Claus, marked the closing on Friday afternoon of Mrs. Pace's Nursery and Kindergarten for the holiday season. The kindergarten rooms located in the Brown Apartment Building were gaily decorated for the occasion, with attention centered on a large spruce Christmas tree. Members of the Rhythm Band gave a performance, and everyone enjoyed singing Yuletide carols, particularly with Santa Claus, who joined the festivities with his usual zest and good humor.

Each child received a gift on behalf of the kindergarten, Joan Bland Jerrell presented one to Santa Claus. Several pictures were taken during the afternoon with refreshments while carrying out the Christmas motif.

Mrs. Frederick Woehr assisted Mrs. Pace in making party arrangements. Before closing for the holidays, Mrs. Pace announced that the Kindergarten and Nursery would re-open for the winter term on January 5th.

In addition to Mrs. Pace and Mrs. Woehr, students attending the party were Nancy Twitty, Dean Vonetes, Bo Tucker, Frances Anthony, Billy Hecht, Gibby Button, Manuel Kolidkis, Stephen Matovich, Jeannie Ford, Katherine Kane, Benjy Holt, Richard Sharpe, Walter Lynn Reynolds, Ruthie Streeter, Buddy Hudgins, Carl Heckie and Terry Lee Jones. Russell Dallas, Edwina Moore, Ronald Lee Harvell, Beverly Wimbish, Angela Miller, Joan Bland Jerrel, Eric Jones, Stephen Moore, Johnny McCabe, Elizabeth Furbush, Linda Sordelette and Joan Huntley. Florence Heckle, Jackie Wotier, Torsten Peterson, Bobby Poole, Willie Szigeti, Skipper Smith, Bobby Elmore, Patricia Norwood, Kenneth Smith, Carol Bruce Clark, Lucinda Pritchard, Ross Cofield, Bob Cassell, Gary Foster, Lawrence Dallas, Sue Ellen Dixon, Allen Sordelette and Ellen Gilliam.

Three students, Michael Mahoney, Frances Halupka and Keith Marks, were unable to attend because of illness.

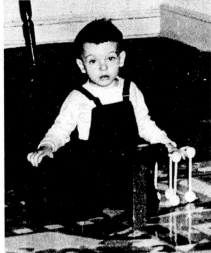

1st Grandson, Thompson G. Pace III

The cheery interior of the back rooms of Mrs. Pace's in City Point Brown
Apartment Building. Thompson G. Pace III is the student.

Inside front Door at Mrs. Pace's

Mrs. Pace with Carla Fay Milton & Mary Elizabeth Bartha in front of
Mrs. Pace's School (Brown Apartments City Point)

Mrs. Patricia Pace, Mrs. Martha Sue Pace, William E. Traylor, Hazel Monroe Traylor, Tina Pace, Tom Pace Sr., Thompson G. Pace III eating a carrot,

Mrs. Pace with Grandson Thompson G. Pace III

You might question, as many parents did, how did Mrs. Pace get the children to have the same interest and excitement in learning as they did in sports? It is unbelievable to think that someone walks in one day and automatically assumes they know how to teach. The student teacher relationship is really based on <u>trust</u>. Many times teachers from later child care centers who had tremendous education visions and ideas did not express them properly to families and found those innovative ideas falling on deaf ears. Many times numerous Hopewell families made the remark that, "Mrs. Pace's was the only children's day-care center to enroll our child."

In grandmother's City Point School, the children would perform their best work, by playing with one another, singing, playing music or acting out dramatic class plays. I have often asked myself, how did grandmother teach a pre-school child to contribute as much energy to their study habits and lesson skills as they would in sports or play? My conclusion is that her lesson plans for children allowed them to make choices, so that they became confident and wanted to do quality work. When children were given responsibility by grandmother, they behaved better. The children did not fear grandmother, who thoughtfully, intelligently, and with a good heart examined that which so many accepted without thinking. The point is, none of us remember the Hopewell News headliners of yesterday like we remember grandmother's school, ideas and teachings. She was no second-rate achiever. She was the best in her field of education at the time. But the applause died, photographs were lost, awards tarnished, achievements were forgotten, and accolades and certificates were buried, until now. She inspired: she taught by example that we are all children of a loving Heavenly Father and that every Goliath can be overcome. She was impactful: Her teachings made a great difference in the lives of many Hopewell citizens. It is my privileged and honor to share these education accomplishments and stories to former students by writing this book.

George H. Donigian, cutting the cake for his birthday, later became a Minister and Editorial Director, Discipleship Resources United Methodist Church.

Thompson G. Pace III on the telephone

Mrs. Pace's daughter, Martha Sue Pace in School

1952—Parasol Dancing: Carol Zillie, Anny Honeycutt, Nancy Tweety,
Ellen Gilliam, Kathy Wallace, Joan Jerrell

1952—"Sailing," a musical play concluded the program, with several children creating a festive mood in colorful costumes, as they sang and danced.

Sailors for this number were Michael Pritchard, Terry Jenks, Steven Korby, Tommy Kirtley, Richard Dolsey
Japanese Girls: Edwina Moore, Elisa Turner, Barbara Pittman, Sandra Walker
Dutch girls: Kathy Sullivan, Margaret Perry, Barbara Strickland, Michele Coxon
Dutch boys: Gary Grundy, Lin Cunningham, Steve Kolidokis, Walter Sheally, Michael Twitty
Uncle Sam: Jimmy Slagle
Parasol Dancing: Carol Zillie, Anny Honrell, Nancy Tweety, Ellen Gilliam, Kathy Wallace, Joan Jerrell

1952—"The Balloon Man," Donald Livingston, Jr., acting as balloon man. Children who came to buy his balloons were Gary Foster, Gregory Harper, Bob Cassell, Manuel Kolidokis, Mike Franklin, Billy Belk, Donald Hagen, Gibby Button, Gordon Walker.

"Sailing," a musical play, concluded the programs, with several children creating a festive mood in colorful costumes, as they sang and danced. Sailors for this number were Michael Pritchard and Terry Walker; Dutch girls: Kathy Sullivan, Margaret Perry, Barbara Strickland, Michele Coxon; Dutch boys: Gary Grundy, Lin Cunningham, Steve Kolidokis, Walter Sheally, Michael Twitty; Uncle Sam: Jimmy Slagle:

1952—Sailor's Swabbing the Deck at Union Hall:

1952—William Wiles Belk, Robert Hershel Cassell, Ann Michele Coxon, Harold Linfield Cunningham, Jr., Richard Lester Dorsey, Gary Randall Grundy, Donald Lee Hagen, Gregory Scott Harper, Terrell Lane Jenks, Thomas Lloyd Kirtley, Jr., Steven Lyle Lorby, Steve Constantine Kolidakis, Donald Ray Livingston, Jr., Margaret Elizabeth Perry, Barbara Jean Pittman, Michael Douglas Pritchard, Walter French Sheally, Jr., James Earl Slagle, Joan Katherine Sullivan, Michael Hendry Twitty, Sandra Eliot Walker

Exercises Held For Mrs. Pace's Kindergarten
(Hopewell News)

The third annual commencement of Mrs. Pace's Kindergarten took place Wednesday evening at the Hopewell High School auditorium before a large, appreciative audience of relatives and friends.

An impressive and unique feature of the commencement this year was the appearance of graduation in caps and gowns, which Mrs. Pace stated was the first time these have been used in kindergarten exercises in the state.

Diplomas Awarded

Diplomas were awarded the **"Graduating Class of 1952"** who having completed the kindergarten course are now ready to enter the first grade next fall. The youngsters, in white caps and gowns, proudly acknowledged this accomplishment, as diplomas were presented them, by moving the tassel on their caps from the left to the right.

The program began with a welcome song, "Take Off Your Troubles and Put On a Smile," by the entire school, resplendent in lavender and white satin band costumes. As four of the group blew bubbles, the others sang "Blowing Bubbles," followed by Bob Cassell in a specialty tap.

Appearing next the Rhythm Band, with all of the children taking part, giving an excellent performance, displaying their training in timing and instrumental harmony, led by Billy Belk as director: Band selections were "Parade of the Wooden Soldiers," "Skaters' Waltz," "The Glow-Worm" and "Slow-Poke."

Youngest Members

Participating next were the youngest members of the kindergarten, who marched, skipped, imitated butterflies in flight, and did a clap, clap number, accompanied by music. "Rhythms" by the older group was also included and they performed as soldiers, elves, high -stepping horse, butterflies, fairies, giants, skaters, ending with a "Clapping Dance."

Characters in a musical play, "The Magic Carpet," were Carholl Zillie, Ann Honeycutt, Nancy Twitty, Ellen Gilliam, Kathy Wallace and Joan Jerrell. Another play, "The Balloon Man," was presented with Donald Livingston, Jr., acting as balloon man. Children who came to buy his balloons were Gary Foster, Gregory Harper, Bob Cassell, Manuel Kolidokis, Mike Franklin, Billy Belk, Donald Hagen, Gibby Button and Gordon Walker.

"Sailing," a musical play concluded the programs, with several children creating a festive mood in colorful costumes, as they sang and danced. Sailors for this number were Michael Pritchard and Terry Walker; Dutch girls: Kathy Sullivan, Margaret Perry, Barbara Strickland, Michele Coxon; Dutch boys: Gary Grundy, Lin Cunningham, Steve Kolidokis, Walter Sheally, Michael Twitty; Uncle Sam: Jimmy Slagle: **Parasol Dancers:** Carol Zillie, Anny Honrell, Ellen Gilliam, and Kathy Wallace.

Graduates

Diplomas were presented to the following students: William Wiles Belk, Robert Hershel Cassell, Anne Michele Coxon, Harold Linfield Cunningham, Jr., Richard Lester Dolsey, Gary Randall Grundy, Donald Lee Hagen, Gregory Scott Harper, Terrell Lane Jenks, Thomas Lloyd Kirtley, Jr., Steven Lyle Korby, Steve Constantine Kilidakis, Donald Ray Livingston, Jr., Margaret Elizabeth Perry, Barbara Jean Pittman, Michael Douglas Pritchard, Walter French Sheally, Jr., James Earl Slagle, Jan Katherine Sullivan, Michael Hendry Twitty, Sandra Eliot Walker.

Staff

Mrs. Thomas Pace and Mrs. Frederick Woehr have conducted the kindergarten during the year. Others on their staff included Mrs. Mary Hepler and Mrs. Dorothy Heffington as substitute teachers and Mrs. H.E. Cassell, pianist.

Serving as ushers for the commencement exercise were Miss Anne Woehr, Miss Jane Crist, Miss Carolyn Dolsey and Miss Margaret Wallace.

While the kindergarten closes officially today to re-open in September, the Nursery Department will remain open next week through June 6. It will close at that time with re-opening planned at present for July 7."

_____***End of Hopewell News Article***_____

Third Annual Commencement

Mrs. Pace's Kindergarten

Presenting

The Graduating Class of 1952

Wednesday, May 28, 1952

Hopewell High School Auditorium

Hopewell, Virginia

Program

Welcome Song—"Take off Your Troubles and Put on a Smile"
By School

Song—"Blowing Bubbles" ------------------------- By School

Top Dance ------------------------------------ Bob Cassell

Rhythm Band ------------------------ Director Billy Belk

Band Selections:
Parade of the Wooden Soldiers   The Glow-worm
Skaters Waltz   Slow Poke

Rhythms ------------------------------ Pre Kindergarten
Skipp
Butterflies
March
Clap Clap Musical

Rhythms ----------------------------------- Kindergarten
Soldiers
Elves
High Stepping Horses
Butterflies
Fairies
Giants
Skaters
A Clapping Dance

A Musical Play—"The Magic Carpet" --------------Caroll Zillie
Ann Honeycutt, Nancy Twitty, Ellen Gilliam
Kathy Wallace, Joan Jerrell

Play—"The Balloon Man" ---- Balloon Man—Donald Livingston
Children—Gary Foster, Gregory Harper, Bob Cassell
Manuel Kolidokis, Mike Franklin, Billy Belk,
Donald Hagen, Gibby Button, Gordon Walker

Musical Play—"Sailing" ---------- Sailors—Michael Pritchard
Terry Jenks, Steven Korby,
Tommy Kirtley, Richard Dolsey.
Japanese Girls ------------ Edwina Moore, Elisa Turner,
Barbara Pittman, Sandra Walker.
Dutch Girls ------------ Kathy Sullivan, Margaret Perry,
Barbara Strickland, Michele Coxon.
Dutch Boys ------------ Gary Grundy, Lin Cunningham
Steve Kolidokis, Walter Sheally, Michael Twitty
Uncle Sam ------------------------------ Jimmy Slagle
Parasol Dancing ----------- Carol Zillie, Ann Honeycutt,
Nancy Tweety, Ellen Gilliam,
Kathy Wallace, Joan Jerrell.

Awarding of Diplomas to

William Wiles Belk

Robert Hershel Cassell

Anne Michele Coxon

Harold Linfield Cunningham, Jr.

Richard Lester Dolsey

Gary Randall Grundy

Donald Lee Hagen

Gregory Scott Harper

Terrell Lane Jenks

Thomas Lloyd Kirtley, Jr.

Steven Lyle Korby

Steve Constantine Kolidakis

Donald Ray Livingston, Jr.

Margaret Elizabeth Perry

Barbara Jean Pittman

Michael Douglas Pritchard

Walter French Sheally, Jr.

James Earl Slagle

Joan Katherine Sullivan

Michael Hendry Twitty

Sandra Eliot Walker

TEACHERS
Mrs. Laura Woehr

Mrs. Thomas Pace

SUBSTITUTE TEACHERS
Mrs. Mary Hepler

Mrs. Dorothy Heffington

PIANIST: Mrs. H. C. Cassell

USHERS
Miss Anne Woehr

Miss Carolyn Dolsey

Miss Jane Crist

Miss Margaret Wallace

1953—Jeanne Ford, Fanny Halupka, Anne Lambert, Terry Lee Jones, Cindy Pritchard, Nancy Rogers, Kathy Kain, Beth Furbush, Ellen Gilliam

Jack-in-Box: Eric Jones
Boy Doll: Steve Moore
Teddy Bear: Andy Hall

1953—Hobo Troubles:

Hoboes with banjoes:...*C.J. Chrzan, Buddy Huggins, Johnny McCabe, Gary Foster, Benji Holt, Billy Hecht, Torsten Peterson;*

Tired Hoboes– That Dance: *Gibby Button, Ronnie Bethea, Carl Heckel, Mike Franklin, Skippy Reynolds, Lee Matovich, Dean Vonetes;*

*1953—The **RHYTHM BAND** from Mrs. Pace's Kindergarten is shown above when they played. Front row, Left to right: Kathy Wallace, Lee Matovish, Ellen Gilliam, Andy Hall, Pat Norwood, Johnnie McCabe, Eddie Huggins, Florence Heckel, Second Row: Beth Furbush, Cindy Pritchard, Ricky Jones, Angela Miller, Stevie Moore, Joan Hundley, Beverley Wimbish, Carl Heckel, Ronnie Bethea, Third Row: Ronald harvell, Ruthie Streeter, Frances Anthony, Gary Foster, Torsten Peterson, Kathy Kain, Mike Mahaney, Benji Holt, Gibby Button, Allan Sordellett, Back Row: Billy Heckt, Terry Lee Jones, Edwina Moore, Anne Lambert, Casmier Chrzan, Dean Vonetes, Skippy Reynolds, Frances Halupka, Jean Ford, Emmanuel Kolidakis.*

1953—Musical Play—A Mischievous fairy with her magic wand makes merry with little girl doll. **Fairy:** Ellen Gilliam, **Dolls:** Kathy Wallace, Beth Furbush, Joan Hundley, Angela Miller, Pat Norwood

A MEDLEY AND DANCE — "Goodnight Ladies" Edwina Moore, Ruthie Streeter, Frances Anthony, Jeanne Ford, Fanny Halupka, Anne Lambert, Terry Lee Jones, Cindy Pritchard, Nancy Rogers, Kathy Kain, Beth Furbush, Kathy Wallace, Ellen Gilliam.

Fanny Halupka, M.Ed. B.S. Teacher

*1953—**Mrs. Pace's Kindergarten** at the holiday with a party at school: Walter Altman, Gordon Walker, Torsten Peterson, Eugene Szigeti, Richard Gill, Michael Gulkis, Kenny Smith, Johnny McCabe, Randy Glass, Bobby Poole, Ronnie Bethea, Eric Jones, Jimmy Mumm, Larry Howell, Robert Kovachaik, Kay Moore, Cheryl Grimsley, Linda Sordelett, Mary Ann Wingold, Deborah Selby, Marcia Johnson; Beverly Wimbish, Barbara Livingston, Cindy Pritchard, Claire Ann Youngblood, Theresa Mathews, Benson Sheally, Anglea Miller, Lynn Matovich, Forence Heckel, Pat Norwood, Judy Rawlings, Douglas Anderson, Bobby Emory, Dorothy Yancey, Kitty Flannagan, Cathy Parker, Micky Minor, Bonnie Broshere, Steve Moore, David Picken and Andy Hail*

Kitty Flannagan-Future Teacher of America..

1953—Musical Play - "When We Grow Up" Grandmother-Fanny Halupka, Grandfather-Michael Mahaney, Mother-Edwina Moore, Father-Emanuel Kolidakis, Young Man-Allan Sordelett, Young Lady-Terry Lee Jones, Little Boy-Ronald Harvell and Little Girl-Kathy Kain

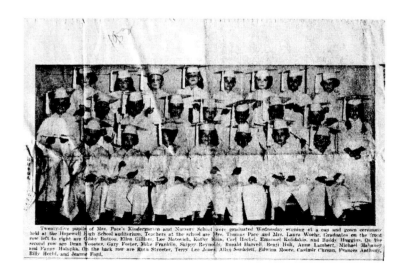

Twenty-five pupils of Mrs. Pace's Kindergarten and Nursery School were graduated Wednesday evening at a cap and gown ceremony held at the Hopewell High School auditorium. Teachers at the school are Mrs. Thomas Pace and Mrs. Laura Woehr. Graduates on the front row left to right are Gibby Button, Ellen Gilliam, Lee Metovich, Kathy Kain, Carl Heckel, Emanuel Kolidakis, and Buddy Huggins. On the second row are Dean Yonetes, Gary Foster, Mike Franklin, Skipey Reynolds, Ronald Harvell, Benji Holt, Anne Lambert, Michael Mahaney and Fanny Halupka. On the back row are Ruth Streeter, Terry Lee Jones, Allan Sordelett, Edwina Moore, Casimir Chrzan, Frances Anthony, Billy Hecht, and Jeanne Ford.

1953 Twenty-five pupils of Mrs. Pace's Kindergarten and Nursery School at the Hopewell High School auditorium. Teachers at the school are Mrs. Thomas Pace and Mrs. Laura Woehr. Graduates on the front row left to right are: Gibby Batton, Ellen Gilliam, Lee Matovich, Kathy Kain, Carl Heckel, Emanuel Kolidakis and Buddy Huggins. Second row: are Dean Vontes, Gary Foster, Mike Franklin, Skippy Reynolds, Ronald Harvett, Benji Holt, Anne Loambert, Michael Mahaney, Fanny Halupka. Third row are Ruth Streeler, Terry Lee Jones, Allan Sordelett, Edwina Moore, Casimir Chrzan, Frances Anthony, Billy Hecht Jeanne Ford

Hopewell School of Childhood

This Certifies that

Frances Seaton Anthony

Having completed the Kindergarten Course of Study is hereby declared Graduate of the Hopewell School of Childhood and awarded this

DIPLOMA

Dated, Hopewell, Virginia, _____ May 27 _____ 19 53

Mrs. Louise Pace Directress

Mrs. Laura Woehr Teacher

Hopewell School of Childhood

Fourth Annual Commencement

Mrs. Pace's Kindergarten and Nursery School

Presenting

The Graduating Class of 1953

Wednesday, May 27, 1953, 8:00 P.M.

Hopewell High School Auditorium

Hopewell, Virginia

PROGRAM

WELCOME SONG — "We Hope You've Brought Your Smiles Along" ---- By School

SONG — "That Doggie In The Window" ---- By School
Quartet — Gibby Button, Billy Hecht, Benji Holt, Michael Mahaney.

SONG — "How Do You Do" ---- By School
Waltzing Girls — Frances Anthony, Jeanne Ford. Anne Lambert. Nancy Rogers, Ruth Streeter.

RHYTHM BAND ---- Director, Allan Sordelett

BAND SELECTIONS — "The First Grade March," "The Parade of the Teddy Bears," "The Petite Waltz.

RHYTHMS ---- Pre-Kindergarten
Skaters, Butterflies, Copy Cat, Skaters   March.

RHYTHMS ---- Kindergarten
Skipping Children, Fairies Running, Birds Flying,, High Stepping Horses, Little Skaters, Clap Clap Dance, Soldiers Marching.

*TAP DANCE — "Varsity Drag" ---- Mary Elizabeth Bartha and Ann Harvell.

MUSICAL PLAY — A mischievous fairy with her magic wand makes merry with a little girl's dolls.
Fairy ---- Ellen Gilliam
Dolls ---- Kathy Wallace, Beth Furbush, Joan Hundley, Angela Miller, Pat Norwood.
Teddy Bear ---- Andy Hall
Bride Doll ---- Cindy Pritchard
Dolls ---- Florence Heckel and Beverly Wimbish
Jack-in-the-Box ---- Eric Jones
Boy Doll ---- Stevie Moore

MUSICAL PLAY — "When We Grow Up"
Grandmother ---- Fanny Halupka
Grandfather ---- Michael Mahaney
Mother ---- Edwina Moore
Father ---- Emanuel Kolidakis
Young Lady ---- Terry Lee Jones
Young Man ---- Allan Sordelett
Little Girl ---- Kathy Kain
Little Boy ---- Ronald Harvell

*TAP DANCE — "Wooden Soldier" ---- Billy Belk

MUSICAL PLAY — "Hobo Troubles
Hoboes with banjoes ---- C. J. Chrzan, Buddy Huggins, Johnny McCabe, Gary Foster, Benji Holt, Billy Hecht, Torsten Peterson.
Tired Hoboes ---- Gibby Button, Ronnie Bethea, Carl Heckel, Mike Franklin, Skippy Reynolds, Lee Matovich, Dean Vonetes.
Dancing Hoboes ---- Gary Foster, Mike Franklin.

A MEDLEY AND DANCE — "Goodnight Ladies"
Edwina Moore, Ruthie Streeter, Frances Anthony, Jeanne Ford, Fanny Halupka, Anne Lambert, Terry Lee Jones, Cindy Pritchard, Nancy Rogers, Kathy Kain, Beth Furbush, Kathy Wallace, Ellen Gilliam.

*TAP DANCE — "Glowworm" ---- Sandy Walker, Dorothy Grainger

*Guests from Olaker School of Dancing

101

Awarding of Diplomas to

FRANCES SEATON ANTHONY

GILBERT LEE BUTTON

CASMIER JOSEPH CHRZAN

MICHAEL ROGER FRANKLIN

JEANNE MARIE FORD

GARY WHEELER FOSTER

ELLEN BLAND GILLIAM

FRANCES KREMER HALUPKA

RONALD LEE HARVELL

WILLIAM JOHN HECHT

CARL BENTON HECKEL

BENJAMIN HARVEY HOLT

EDWARD DeWITT HUGGINS

TERRY LEE JONES

KATHLEEN MARY KAIN

EMANUEL NICOLAS KOLIDAKIS

ANNE TILMAN LAMBERT

MICHAEL LEE MAHANEY

STEPHEN LeGRANDE MATOVICH

EDWINA LEE MOORE

ALLAN KARNES SORDELETT

RUTH PRITCHETT STREETER

WALTER LYNN REYNOLDS

NANCY WEEKS ROGERS

DEAN ALFRED VONETES

TEACHERS

Mrs. Laura Woehr   **Mrs. Thomas Pace**

SUBSTITUTE TEACHERS

Mrs. Mary Hepler   **Mrs. Ann Harvell**

Pianist—Mrs. P. M. Grainger, Jr.
Lighting—Alton Crist

USHERS

Miss Jane Crist   Miss Laurie Wallace
Miss Bessie Norwood   Miss Anne Woehr

1954 —"One Umbrella Built for Two" Theresa Mathieu, Willie Szigeti, Marsha Johnson, Walter Aultman, Linda Sordelett, Robert Kovschak, Barbara Livingston, Johnny McCabe, Beverly Aldridge, Michael Gulkis

1954—Stephen Moore, Ronnie Brashear; **Bunny:** Monique Minor, Pat Norwood, Lynn Matovich, Judy Rawlings, Barbara Barber

A Dance with Tambourines: Claire Ann Youngblood, Jackie Ann Harris, Debby Selby, Cindy Pritchard, Mary Ann Wingold

1954—Bunny Cottontail: Monique Minor
1st Bunny Judy Rawlings, 1st girl from left Pat Norwood
Peter Cottontail: Benson Sheally

1954 "Umbrella Built For Two" Theresa Mathieu, Willie Szigeti, Marsha Johnson, Walter Aultman, Linda Sordelett, Robert Kovschak, Barbara Livingston, Johnny McCabe, Beverly Aldridge, Michael Gulkis

1954 Jimmy Mumm, Beverly Aldridge, Larry Wayne Howell

A BARBERSHOP SEXTETTE— On Moonlight Bay, Sidewalks of New York, In The Good Old Summer Time and Heart of My Heart

Left to Right:

1954—
Kenny Smith, Torsten Edward Peterson, Jr., Attorney-At-Law Hopewell, Virginia, Gordon Walker, Randy Glass, Bobby Pooler, Richard Gill, M.B.S, William & Mary– Director of Mathematics Rappahannock Community College

1954—The Rhythm Band

Beverly Wimbish Aldridge, Walter Moore Altman, III., Richard Woolridge Gill, George Randolph Glass, Michael Frederick Gulkis, Larry Wayne Howell, Marsha Jane Johnson, Eric Yallowly Jones, Robert Anthony Kovschak, Barbara Ann Livingston, Theresa Louise Mathieu, John Stanley McCabe, Jr., James Elwyn Mumm, Robert Temple Poole, Deborah Ann Selby, Kenneth Michael Smith, Linda Louise Sordelett, Eugene Szigeti, Jr, Torsten Edward Peterson, Jr., Lucinda Lee Pritchard, Gordon Willis Walker, Jr., Mary Ann Wingold, Claire Ann Youngblood

1954—Graduates Mrs. Pace's School

Awarding of diplomas to: Beverly Wimbish Aldridge, Walter Moore Aultman, III., Richard Woolridge Gill, George Randolph Glass, Michael Frederick Gulkis, Larry Wayne Howell, Marsha Jane Johnson, Eric Yallowly Jones, Robert Anthony Kovschak, Barbara Ann Livingston, Theresa Louise Mathieu, John Stanley McCabe, Jr., James Elwyn Mumm, Robert Temple Poole, Deborah Ann Selby, Kenneth Michael Smith, Linda Louise Sordelett, Eugene Szigeti, Jr, Torsten Edward Peterson, Jr., Lucinda Lee Pritchard, Gordon Willis Walker, Jr., Mary Ann Wingold, Claire Ann Youngblood

Hopewell School of Childhood

Fifth Annual Commencement

Mrs. Pace's Kindergarten and Nursery School

Presenting

The Graduating Class of 1954

Wednesday, May 26, 1954,   8:00 P.M.

Hopewell High School Auditorium

Hopewell, Virginia

Program

WELCOME SONG — "We're Mighty Glad You Came" _____ School

SONG — "Smiles" _____ School

RHYTHM BAND _____ Director, Kenneth Smith
    "Little Ensign March" _____ Giese
    "Parade of the Wooden Soldiers" _____ Jessell
    "The Skaters' Waltz" _____ Richter

RHYTHMS _____ Nursery School
    Skipping, Butterflies, Skating, "My Shadow", March.

DANCE — "The Hokey Pokey" _____ School

RHYTHMS _____ Kindergarten Boys
    Soldiers Marching, Funny Giraffes, The Big Train, Giants Walking,
    Elephants, Indians Dancing, Little Fishermen.

RHYTHMS _____ Kindergarten Girls
    Fairies Dancing, Butterflies, Wooden Dolls, Skaters, Skipping Children,
    "Here We Come A-Walking."

* DANCE — "The Little Toe Dancer" _____ Mary Elizabeth Bartha, Dollie
    Anne Lewis.

DRAMATIZED SONGS _____ Chorus
    "School Days" _____ Pat Norwood, Bobby Emory, Lynn Matovich,
    Dwight Lee, Judy Rawlings, Steve Moore, Monique Minor, Danny Coe,
    Barbara Barber, Ronnie Brashear.
    "Little Hans" _____ Michael Gulkis
    "Where Did You Get That Hat?" _____ Eric Jones
    "I Don't Want To Play in Your Yard" _____ Beverly Aldridge
    Larry Howell, Jimmy Mumm.

A DANCE WITH TAMBOURINES ——
    Claire Ann Youngblood, Jackie Ann Harris, Debby Selby, Cindy
    Pritchard, Mary Ann Wingold.

TAP DANCE — "Paper Doll" _____ Monique Minor

"WORKING ON THE RAILROAD" _____ Ronnie Brasher, Robbie Elswine,
    Benson Sheally, Danny Coe, Steve Moore, Dwight Lee, Bobby Emory.

* TAP DANCE — "You're The Cream In My Coffee" _____ Olivia Johnson,
    Sandra Walker.

A BARBERSHOP SEXTETTE — "Heart of My Heart" _____ Richard Gill,
    Randy Glass, Bobby Poole, Torsten Peterson, Kenny Smith, Gordon
    Walker.

SONG — "One Umbrella Built For Two" _____ Theresa Mathieu, Willie
    Szigeti, Marsha Johnson, Walter Aultman, Linda Sordelett, Robert
    Kovschak, Barbara Livingston, Johnny McCabe, Beverly Aldridge,
    Michael Gulkis.

"PETER AND BUNNY COTTONTAIL AND THEIR FRIENDS" —
    Bunny Cottontail _____ Monique Minor
    Peter Cottontail _____ Benson Sheally
    Friends _____ Steve Moore, Ronnie Brashear,
    Pat Norwood, Lynn Matovich, Judy Rawlings, Barbara Barber.

WALTZ — "The Merry Widow Waltz" ---------- Gordon Walker — Theresa
    Mathieu, Willie Szigeti — Mary Ann Wingold, Bobby Emory — Pat
    Norwood, Walter Aultman — Cindy Pritchard, Robert Kovschak —
    Marsha Johnson, Johnny McCabe — Linda Sordelett, Bobby Poole —
    Jackie Ann Harris, Torsten Peterson — Debby Selby, Larry Howell —
    Claire Ann Youngblood, Michael Gulkis — Beverly Aldridge.

SONG — "Baby Talk" -------- Words and music were written by Mrs. Pace
    for her grandsons and dedicated to all young mothers.
    Beverly Aldridge, Jackie Ann Harris, Marsha Johnson, Barbara Living-
    ston, Theresa Mathieu, Monique Minor, Pat Norwood, Cindy Pritchard,
    Judy Rawlings.

* TAP DANCE — "Take Me Out To The Ball Game" ------ Frances Anthony,
    Billy Belk.

AWARDING OF DIPLOMAS ——

Awarding of Diplomas to

BEVERLY WIMBISH ALDRIDGE

WALTER MOORE AULTMAN, III

RICHARD WOOLRIDGE GILL

GEORGE RANDOLPH GLASS

MICHAEL FREDERICK GULKIS

LARRY WAYNE HOWELL

MARSHA JANE JOHNSON

ERIC YALLOWLY JONES

ROBERT ANTHONY KOVSCHAK

BARBARA ANN LIVINGSTON

THERESA LOUISE MATHIEU

JOHN STANLEY McCABE, JR.

JAMES ELWYN MUMM

ROBERT TEMPLE POOLE

DEBORAH ANN SELBY

KENNETH MICHAEL SMITH

LINDA LOUISE SORDELETT

EUGENE SZIGETI, JR.

TORSTEN EDWARD PETERSON, JR.

LUCINDA LEE PRITCHARD

GORDON WILLIS WALKER, JR.

MARY ANN WINGOLD

CLAIRE ANN YOUNGBLOOD

* Guests from Olaker School of Dancing

1954
TEACHERS

Mrs. Laura Woehr   Mrs. Louise Pace

SUBSTITUTE TEACHERS

Mrs. Mary Hepler   Mrs. Sue Jones

PIANIST—Mrs. Ivan Christoffel

LIGHTING—Alton Crist

USHERS

Melissa Aderholt   Bessie Norwood
Jane Crist   Carol Stevens
Connie Douglas   Anne Woehr

Martha Sue Pace Traylor with 1st child, William Ellsworth Traylor, Jr.
Mrs. Patricia Louise Pace's second grandson.

Hobo Troubles—Tired Hoboes—Dancing Hoboes

(1953) Photo taken in Mrs. Pace's house 208 Ramsey Avenue.
Frances Seaton Anthony always loved being a witch, gathering each year at grandmother's.

117

Each year when Halloween arrived, Mrs. Pace would invite all the school & neighborhood children to come by and have their pictures taken.

Robert "Rocky" Anderson III and Mrs. Pace's 2nd grandson, William Ellsworth Traylor Jr.

1955—John Marchington Altman, Robert Richardson Emory, Clemant William Halupka, Mark Robert Harrison, Archer Lee Jones, William Keith Marks, Stephen Fenner Moore, John Henry Pope, and Billy Albert Wilding

Hopewell City Fire Department

Pace Kindergarten Has Treat Party

The Hopewell School of Childhood celebrated Halloween with black cats and witches in the gallery decorated rooms of Mrs. Pace's Kindergarten and Nursery School.

Mrs. William Merner and Mrs. T.G. Pace entertained the children with a party on October 29. The children in costumes sang songs of Halloween and played games. Refreshments were served and each of the children was given a bag of candy with a ginger bread boy and a pirates hat.

Those enrolled in the school are: Johnny Altman, Susan Allen, Gregg Andrews, Delmer Coe, Susan Abernathy, Susan Cerrito, Robert Emory, Frances Ford, Lou Brenda Haile, Sandra Sacra, Clement Halupka, Jackie Harris Florence Heckley, Susan Kain, Dwight Lee and Lynn Matovich. Also, Keith Marks, Mary Elizabeth McPheeters, Patricia Norwood, Dianne Patterson, John H. Pope Jr., Linda Spatig, Allen Sprinkle, Mark Harrison, Dora Greery, Betty Rollings, Don Andrews, George Donigian, Robert Drule, Skippy-Drurie, William Garvin, Moneque Minor, Kathryn Parker, David Pickens, Judy Rawlings, Benson Sheally, Virginia Szigeti, Thomas Walker, Carlton Webb, Dorothy Yancy and Ricky Shallenburger.

After school nursery students are: Cindy Pritchard, Mary Bartha, Beverly Aldridge, and Ellen Gilliam. Kindergarten students of the Hopewell School of Childhood pause in their play to don their new pirate hats and other costumes at a party recently at the school. Mrs. T.G. Pace and Mrs. William Merner are their teachers.

Pace Kindergarten Registration Set
(Hopewell News)

Registration for Mrs. Pace's Kindergarten Nursery School and Day Care will be held at her home at 208 Ramsey Avenue, on Tuesday July 20 from 10 to 12 A. M. and from 3 until 5 P.M.

Mrs. Mary Agnes Merner will assume duties as the kindergarten teacher when the school reopens. A graduate from East Carolina Teachers College, she was a first grade teacher at DuPont School for five years.

Mrs. Merner is the wife of William L. Merner, teacher and coach at Hopewell High School.

_____***End of Hopewell News Article***_____

Mrs. Mary Agnes Merner was Mrs. Pace's second Kindergarten Teacher in the early 1950's. Hopewell's football stadium is named **"Merner Field."**

WILLIAM L. MERNER
A.B.
East Carolina Teachers' College
Commercial, Coach

Mrs. Mary Agnes Merner
East Carolina Teachers' College

HOPEWELL SCHOOL OF CHILDHOOD

SIXTH ANNUAL COMMENCEMENT

MRS. PACE'S KINDERGARTEN & NURSERY SCHOOL

PRESENTING

The Graduating Class of 1955

Friday, May 27, 1955—10:20 A. M.

Brown Apartments

Hopewell, Virginia

PROGRAM

WELCOME SONG,

"Take Off Your Worry and Put on a Smile"

By School

SONG,

"If I Knew You Were Coming I'd Have Baked a Cake"

By School

RHYTHM BAND,   Director, Susan Abernathy

BAND SELECTION, Baa, Baa, Black Sheep, Twinkle Twinkle
Little Star, Alexander's Ragtime Band, Let the Sun Shine In.

THE RHYTHM SKIT-SKATS

Bob Durio, Carlton Webb, Tommy Walker, Neal Arnold, Ritchie Molianson,
Robert Moliason, Ricky Shallenberger.

IN FAIRY LAND   Fairy Queen, Judy Rawling
FARIES: Lynn Matovich, Betty Rawling, Sandra Sacra,
            Donna   Creery.

COWBAY ROUNDUP   —   Kindergarten
Let Me Wa—Hoo, Square Dance, Oh, Suzanna,
Tweedle—Deedle—Deedle—Dee, This Old School.

TEDDY BEARS ON PARADE

Skipper Durie, Bob Durie, Carlton Webb, Tommy Walker, Neal Arnold,
Ritchie Moliason, Ricky Shallenberger, Robert Moliason,

AWARDING OF DIPLOMAS TO

Susan Dianne Abernathy
John Marchington Alton
Susan Marie Cerrito
Delmer Lee Coe
Donna Rae Creery
Robert Richardson Emory
Frances West Ford
Clemant William Halupka
Jacky Ann Harris
Mark Robert Harrison
Florence Gurnsey Heckle
Archer Lee Jones
Susan Ann Kain
Mary Elizabeth Kay McPheetoers
Virginia Lynn Matovick
William Keith Marks
Stephon Fonner Moore
Patricia Norwood
Dianne Dale Patterson
John Henry Pope
Elizabeth Jean Rollings
Linda Spatig
Billy Albert Wilding   SONG—AMERICA

TEACHERS

Mrs. Mary Agnes Merner

Mrs. Louise Pace

SUBSTITUTE TEACHERS

Mrs. Mary Hepler   Mrs. Betty Lewis

Mrs. John Spatig

PIANIST

Mrs. John Spatig

125

SCHOOL OPENING

HOPEWELL SCHOOL OF CHILDHOOD

HOPEWELL SCHOOL OF CHILDHOOD

Dear Patron:

The Hopewell School of Childhood will begin its EIGHTH session on Tuesday September 4, 1956.

This is to advise that I am saving a reservation for your child and you will find your enrollment blank enclosed. If for any reason you will not need the reservation, please advise me promptly by calling CE—2846—otherwise bring it with you Thursday, August 30. There will be no school Monday, September 3, but patrons are asked to bring their children, complete their enrollment, and visit the schoolroom, Thursday, August 30, from 10 to 12 a.m. and from 4 to 5 p.m. It is requested that all hats, coats, leggings, gloves, galoshes and lunch box or bag be plainly marked with the child's name. This is necessary because very young children do not recognize their possessions among so many similar ones.

Every morning at ten thirty we have our "Tea Party" period. The children bring a very light lunch from home and during this time they are taught table etiquette and social adjustment with a group.

It is possible for your child to bring us a cold as well as get one from contact with us. So, if your child has a cold, please keep him/her at home for 48 hours or until he/she is sufficiently well to be with other children. Should your child be exposed to any of the children's diseases, if you would tell me immediately, I can advise you about the incubation period and when to keep him/her isolated.

If we work together, I feel sure that we will have a happier, healthier group of children.

We will have four parties for the year, Halloween, Christmas, Valentine and Easter. Please do not send gifts for Christmas.

Tuition for kindergarten and nursery school is $10.00 a month to be paid the first of each month as long as enrolled. Transportation is $5.00 a month to be paid with tuition.

I pledge you my loyalty for a happy year with your child and thank you for the joyous privilege.

Sincerely yours,

Louise Pace

(Mrs.) Louise Pace

1956—Children from Mrs. Pace's kindergarten and nursery school are pictured here when they visited the Hopewell Fire Department on Thursday. In the picture not in order are Bobby Hecht, Phillip Rodgers, Virginia Szigeti, Rolland Hazlitte, Diane Dalton, Douglas Pritchard, Jr., Gilliam Peterson, Peter Leadbetter, Nancy Kain, Allen Flannagan, Paige Barker, Margaret Ford, Becky Kanak, Helen Pross, Bill Carter, Leslie Foley, Linda Balays, Gail Magruder, Roy Allen, Judy Rollins, Skipper Durie, Stephen Maxwell, Carol Livingston, Ricky Roth, Carl Hughes, Laura Beth Adams, Robert Anderson, John Barton, Jr., Jeffery Bortnicker, Billy Chivers, Carolyn Coe, George Donigian, Robert Durie, Faith Heckle, James Holt, Phillip Maxwell, Nancy Michers, Marshall Minchers, Steven Selinger, Kerin Swinehart, Clayton Turetta, Ross Thornley, Tommy Walker, Becky Swicegood, Billy Traylor, Karen Chiners, Cynthia Jane Wood

Mrs. Pace, Martha Sue Pace, Mrs. Furr, and Mrs. Barber

1956—Cowboys—Robert Hecht, Leslie Foley, Philip Rogers, Richard Roth, Stephen Maxwell, Carl Hughes, Douglas Pritchard, Allen Flannagan, Paige Barker, Tommy Carter, Rayland Hazelette, Peter Leadbetter, Bub Gilliam, Eddie Wills

1956—Carola Alter, Weldon Paige Barker, Linda Constance Balozs, Janice Corrine Brogdon, Karen Mae Chivers, William Thomas Carter, Samuel P. Durie, Dianne Gail Dalton, Frank Leslie Foley, Margaret Lee Ford, Allen Wadell Flannagan, III, Roland Chris Hazalette, Jr., Robert Roland Hecht, Carl Weston Hughes, Rebecca Estelle Kanak, Peter Irby Leadbetter, Stephen Perrine Maxwell, Gail Benner Magruder, Gillian Ragland Peterson, Luther Douglas Pritchard, Jr., Helen Laurelle Pross, Judy Lynne Rawlings, Phillip B. Rogers, Richard A. Roth, Virginia Szigeti, Kay Archer Tucker, Monique Renne Minor, and Paula Elaine Owens

Thelma "Olaker's School of Dance" program at Hercules Union Hall; Thelma Olaker choreographed all Mrs. Pace's dramatic productions in the 40's, 50's and early to mid 60's.

THELMA OLAKER
YOUTH CIVIC BALLET COMPANY

Thelma Olaker and Daughter—Christin

Presented by Senior, Junior and Apprentice Ballet Company members.

ARTISTIC DIRECTOR...............Christin Parks
BALLET MISTRESS.................Karmon Martin
CHOREOGRAPHY....................Christin Parks

Thelma Olaker was quintessentially an old-school ballet teacher. She was a fresh spirit rose, who wore red lipstick and smoked cigarettes. Grandmother's Kindergarten and Nursery School dance training can be traced to her dedicated and well established "Olaker's School of Dance." Mrs. Thelma Olaker choreographed all of Mrs. Pace's dance and dramatic shows later to be carried on by her daughter, Christin Parks. Dance recitals were taught and preformed on Hopewell's Hercules Union Hall stage as well as Patrick Copeland Elementary School and Hopewell High School.

Advertised on all Mrs. Pace's dramatic school play production programs from her first in 1950 was **"Thelma Olaker School of Dance."**

* Guests from Olaker School of Dancing

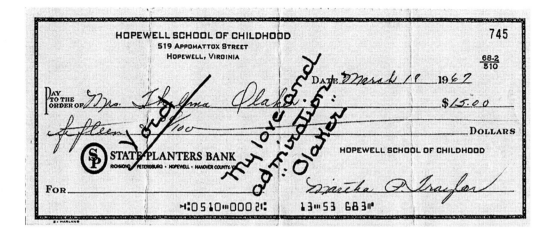

Mother and Father shared this story about Thelma Olaker's School of Dance. "Thelma Olaker's was next door to Mrs. Pace's school in the Brown Apartments across from City Point Inn. If anything ever happened to Thelma's pianist, she would run over to Grandmother's school; she was tiny and would flutter her hands up and down in the air saying, "What am I going to do Mrs. Pace? I don't have anyone to play piano for me." Grandmother said, "First calm down and let me get my children settled and Sue can stay here while I come over and play for you." Mother told Billy and me, "That's how you both got your dancing lessons and cotillion for free. When I sent Thelma a check, she would always send it back, VOID." They were truly close friends.

Mother: "when the school started , it was called Pacy's," Father begins to talk, "Bill you weren't there, you were overseas. I don't know where he was, probably in Hartford Connecticut with that beautiful girl he always tell's me about. We lived close to City Point Inn, and that's where all the solders wives lived when they came here. Right across the bridge is where we lived, on the corner. Daddy had a great big garden. And these pretty little girls would come by, and Daddy was just like uncle Tom, and Bobby, when they saw a pretty girl, they said, "Honey, come here and let me give you some vegetables to take home and cook tonight."

Robert: In my education research study it shows that kids who eat school breakfast miss fewer school days.

Mother: The privates only got $21.00 dollars a month. So, they could use it. Daddy fed everybody, half of City Point; we got to know them and they all had little children.

Well, they'd come over and Daddy and Mother loved children. They'd say, "I've got to go out to Fort Lee tonight and I don't know what I'm going to do with the children, and Daddy would say, "bring um over here we'll keep um." They'd bring um in a carriage and keep one or two at a time. And they'd come back and pick them up. We got so involved, Mother said, "I might as well have a little nursery school here in the backyard, just in the mornings." And she charged 10 cents an hour to keep the children. She had a little High School girl to help her.

Father: I don't remember that.

Mother: You were in France, I think, or Hartford, one or the other. Anyway, she had little cards printed. Sometimes she would have twenty-five to thirty children in the morning playing out in the backyard, but it was all enclosed. Everybody loved Pacy. Daddy and Mother were Pacy's. It was just Pacy's Nursery school. Then she decided she was going to keep them all day. She charged $10.00 a week to keep them all day. We kept them in the house on Ramsey Avenue, until Daddy died in 1948.

Father: That's when we were married in, 1949.

Mother: Granddaddy was 59, but all the records show he was in his sixties.

Father: People back in those days had to lie about their age to get a job.

Mother: When they were forty they let you go.

Father: After you passed forty, they didn't want you.

Mother: He was a pipe fitter Supervisor for "Tubies," which was Celanese later. We could have gone to South America when the plant was transferred down there, but Mother got sick and we didn't go. Then Mother decided after Daddy died that she would rent a building and have a Kindergarten and Nursery School and all-day care. Laura Woehr, was her first Kindergarten teacher. Mother taught the younger ones, and Mrs. Olaker, you know Mrs. Olaker who taught you and your brother both how to dance. She was right next-door, and we stayed in the Brown Apartments and we had the first private Kindergarten in City Point.

Father: Actually Bobby the business went into sort of commercial operations in 1951, The Internal Revenue Forms I had to send in, for the Day Care Center were1951. It was a sole proprietorship. No reason to incorporate and repay a fee every year. We had liability insurance on it.

Mother: We were licensed by the state and that was free.

Father: We weren't big enough to incorporate. A corporation charter cost a lot of money and you had to renew it every year.

Mother: We were licensed by the state, and that didn't cost you anything either. Your Grandmother always said, "live and let live," that's why we didn't make any money.

Father: What was the name of the teacher that Louise Spatig's sister taught one year? Bill Merner's wife, Mary after that, and then the preacher's wife and many, many more. Carl Flack was a wonderful teacher. Diddy Flannagan and Mother wrote some wonderful plays and should have had them copyrighted. "The Wise Old Owl" should have been copyrighted and published.

Mother: Diddy and I wrote that one.

Father: When they had the closing exercises down at Patrick Copland, Plato Eliades was there that night with his children He told Sue, "You could sell tickets to this thing and make money. If you have it again you could sell tickets for $5.00 apiece," and $5.00 was a lot of money back then.

Mother said: You have seen it one time for free and you'll never see it again, because it was hard work. But, don't let anyone ever tell you that little children can't act and sing. Mother humbled herself as she did often, by saying, I couldn't sing and couldn't play, but I could discipline, and I did. My mother could sing and play I have her singing and playing on video. She was wonderful.

Father: I'll never forget the kids were lined up on the stage right close together and Don Gargus in personnel at Allied Chemical his daughter came up on stage and she was looking for a place to stand and push two children apart and she said, "Get over." The house came down. She was the one who went out on stage, and no one ever prompted the children; they prompted each other. They knew each other's parts. She was the most adorable little girl you have ever seen. See walked out into the middle of the stage and said, "I have to go to the bathroom."

Mother: I had to walk out on stage to get her and take her off.

Pajama Play Rehearsal

135

Music lessons at Union Hall

More tap dancing lessons by Thelma Olaker at Hercules Union Hall
with Mrs. Pace's children

Thelma "Olaker's School of Dance"& "Mrs. Pace's" children at Hercules Union Hall:
Ballet and tap dancing lessons.

Mrs. Olaker's dance rehearsal and lessons at Union Hall.

"Varsity Drag" with Mary Elizabeth Bartha and Ann Harvell

1956—Carola Alter, Weldon Paige Barker, Linda Constance Balozs, Janice Corrine Brog-don, Karen Mae Chivers, William Thomas Carter, Samuel P. Durie, Dianne Gail Dalton, Frank Leslie Foley, Margaret Lee Ford, Allen Wadell Flannagan, III, Roland Chris Hazalette, Jr., Robert Roland Hecht, Carl Weston Hughes, Rebecca Estelle Kanak, Peter Irby Leadbetter, Stephen Perrine Maxwell, Gail Benner Magruder, Gillian Ragland Peter-son, Luther Douglas Pritchard, Jr., Helen Laurelle Pross, Judy Lynne Rawlings, Phillip B. Rogers, Richard A. Roth, Virginia Szigeti, Kay Archer Tucker, Monique Renne Minor, and Paula Elaine Owens

Christin Olaker Parks

Hopewell School of Childhood

Seventh Annual Commencement

Mrs. Pace's Kindergarten
and Nursery School

Presenting

The Graduating Class of 1956

THURSDAY, MAY 24, 1956 7:30 P.M.

UNION HALL—10TH AND BROADWAY

HOPEWELL, VA.

PROGRAM

WELCOME SONG—We Hope You've Brought Your Smiles
Along .... SCHOOL

RHYTHM BAND—Kindergarten—Director, Becky Kanak
"Way Down in George" "Waltz" "March"

RHYTHMS .... Nursery School

Ponies, Butterflies, Skating, My Shadow, Clap—
Clap, Little Fisherman, March
SONG: Green and Red Box

COWBOY DRILL .... Kindergarten

Robert Hecht—Leslie Foley—Phillip Rogers
Richard Roth—Stephen Maxwell—Carl Hughes
Douglas Pritchard—Allen Flannagan—Paige
Barker—Tommy Carter—Rayland Hazelette—
Peter Leadbetter—Bub Gilliam—Eddie Mills

RHYTHM BAND .... Nursery School

Twinkle, Twinkly Little Star
Doggie In The Window
Happy Birthday

DRAMATIZED SONG—..........................Kindergarten

"Mary Contrary's Garden
Marys: Becky Kanak—Diane Dalton—Virginia
Szigeti—Judy Rawling—Gail Magruder
Monique Minor—Gillian Peterson

Flowers: Janice Brogdon—Kay Tucker—Karen
Chivers—Margaret Ford—Helen Pross
Carola Alter—Linda Balozs

THE NAVY ON PARADE .... Kindergarten
DRAMATIZED SONG — "Blowing Bubbles"

Bubble Girls: Paula Owens—Virginia Szigeti
Judy Rawlings

| CHORUS: | .... | Kindergarten |
| **GRANDFATHER'S DREAM** | .... | Kindergarten |

Grandfather: Samuel Durie

Grandfather's Girl: Helen Pross

School Teacher: Stephen Maxwell

Chorus

DRAMATIZED SONG .... Nursery School

"Winking—Blinkin and Nod"
Robert Durie—Tommy Walker—Billy Chivers
George Donigian—Philip Maxwerll—Steve
Selenger—Ross Thornsley—Carolyn Coe
Nancy Meyers—Becky Swicegood—Clayton Terretta

AWARDING OF DIPLOMAS: -TO—

CAROLA ALTER

WELDON PAIGE BARKER

LINDA CONSTANCE BALOZS

JANICE CORRINE BROGDON

KAREN MAE CHIVERS

WILLIAM THOMAS CARTER

SAMUEL P DURIE

DIANNE GAIL DALTON

FRANK LESLIE FOLEY

MARGARET LEE FORD

ALLEN WADELL FALNNAGAN, III

ROLAND CHRIS HAZALETTE, JR.

ROBERT ROLAND HECHT

CARL WESTON HUGHES

REBECCA ESTELLE KANAK

PETER IRBY LEADBETTER

STEPHEN PERRINE MAXWELL

GAIL BENNER MAGRUDER

GILLIAN RAGLAND PETERSON

LUTHER DOUGLAS PRITCHARD

HELEN LAURELLE PROSS

JUDY LYNNE RAWLINGS

PHILLIP B ROGERS

RICHARD A ROTH

VIRGINIA SZIGETI

KAY ARCHER TUCKER

MONIQUE RENNE MINOR

PAULA ELAINE OWENS

1956 TEACHERS

MRS. MURIEL MILTON MRS. ALICE SZIGETI
MRS. LOUISE PACE

SUBSTITUTE TEACHERS

Mrs. Mary Hepler, Mrs. Betty Lewis, Mrs. Lydia Fisher

PIANIST: Mrs. Muriel Milton & Mrs. Louise Pace

1957—It was happy time at the Hopewell School of Childhood when a party was held to celebrate four birthdays. Those who were honored were Anne Mabrey, Neil Biltzer, Martha Sordelette, and William Garvin. Pupils to help celebrate the occasion were Jimmie Hart, Faith Heckle, Phillip Maxwell, Marshall Minshew, Rozella Jo Cain, Joan Hangella, Roger Hughes, Sandra Lewis, Carol Madren, Johnny McBride, Stephen McGuire, Ceccilla Joseph, Billy Traylor, Chuck Jerell, Ross Thorney, George Edwards, Margaret Nelson, Daniella Aderholt, James Alford, Jeffery Bartniker, Barbara Buys, Robert Dail, George Donigion, Robert Durie, Rebecca Hampton, Ligon Jones, Paula Lewis, Michael McGuire, William Mitchell, Timothy Moore, Elizabeth Peterson, Patricia Podlewski, Robert Reeves, Ricky Shallenger, Clayton Terrerin, Tommy Walker, David Youngblood, Rebecca Swiergood, Lona Lee Lyons with Mrs. Linda Fisher, Mrs. Louise Pace, Mrs. William Traylor assist in serving the young guest.

Brenda Sue Allen **1957**

May 1957, Brenda Sue Allen in school square dance.
Note: The lipstick was for her stage performance!

1957—*Danielle Lee Aderholt, James Bruce Alford, Neil David Blitzer, Jeffrey Bortniker, Raymond Lee Drake, Ronnie Phillip Chapman, Robert Lynn Dail, George Donigian, Robert A Durie Rebecca Arnette Hampton, Ligon Loflin Jones, Paula Anne Lewis Elizabeth Hill Peterson, William Luther Mitchell, Patricia Ann Podlewski, Cindy Jane Shuford, Martha Louise Sordelett, David Craig Youngblood, Willaim Colquitt Garvin, Barbara Catherine Buys, Rebecca Susan Swicegood, Ross Frazer Thornley, Gail Magruder, Timothy Moore*

1957—"Do the Bunny Hop" Cindy Shuford, Libby Peterson, Gail Magruder, Martha Sordelette, Joan Hangello—**White Bunny:** Sandy Lewis

Bunnies on Parade: Bunny Hop Tap Dancing

Hopewell School of Childhood

Eighth Annual Commencement

Presenting

The Graduating Class of 1957

FRIDAY, MAY 24, 1957 8:00 P.M.

Hopewell High School Auditorium

Hopewell, Virginia

PROGRAM

WELCOME   Billy Garvin

SMILES   SONG BY THE SCHOOL

WELCOME SONG— "We Hope You Brought Your Smiles Along"
                                             SONG BY THE SCHOOL

DANCE   A WALTZ

BY: Gilliam Peterson, Mary Kelly, Peggy Sordelette,
Becky Kanak, Jameil Ameen, Virginia Szigetti

RHYTHM BAND   By the Kindergarten

Director: Robert Durie
Selections: Winter Wonderland, Georgia Camp Meeting, Waltz

RHYTHMS   By the Nursery School

Galloping, Butterflies, Skating, Clap—Clap,
A Fishing We will Go, March

RHYTHM BAND   By the Nursery School

Director: Jimmy Holt

Selections: Baa Baa Black Sheep, Jingle Bells,
                        Dark Town Strutters Ball

LITTLE BOY BLUE

Boy Blue	Jeffrey Bostnicker
Helpers:	George Donigian, Neal Blitzer, Ronnie Chapman, Robert Durie, Ross Thornsley, Philip Maxwell, James Alford, Raymond Drake

*Guest from Olaker School of Dancing

"RAINCOAT"   Nursery School Boys

DANCE   Joan Hangello and
                   Margaret Nelson

"THEY ALWAYS PICK ON ME"   Sung by Marshall Minchew

BUNNY HOP

Bunnies: Cindy Shuford, Libby Peterson,
Gail Magruder, Martha Sordelette, Joan Hangello

White Bunny: Sandy Lewis

DANCE ..   "Rocky Bye Baby" and "Hi Diddle Diddle"
                Sandy Lewis, Amy Mabry, Karan Smith, Louise
                Whitt, Antonette Kee

"ONE UMBRELLA BUILT FOR TWO"   Sung By:
Rebecca Hampton, Lucky Jones, Paula Lewis,
Robbie Dail, Rebecca Swicegood, Billy Mitchell
Patricia Podlewski, David Youngblood, Barbara Buys,
Timothy Moore.

BUY A BALLOON   By the Nursery School

Balloon Man: Jimmy Holt
Buyers: Sandy Lewis, Karan Smith, Ann Mabry
            Billy Traylor, Roger Hughes, Antonette Kee
            Chuck Jerrell, George Edwards, Jonny
            McBride, Joan Hangello, Margaret Nelson
            Lane Prichard, Marshall Minchew, Louise
            Whitt

| **HOBOS** | A Dramatized Song by the Kindergarten Boys |
| **DANCE** | A WALTZ |

* Guest of the Olaker School of Dancing

MARY CONTRARY'S GARDEN

MARYS: Becky Hampton, Paula Lewis, Gail Magruder, Libby Peterson, Patricia Podlewski

FLOWERS: Becky Swicegood, Cindy Shuford, Martha Sordelette, Barbara Buys, Joan Hangello

All Costumes Furnished by the School

AWARDING OF DIPLOMAS

DANIELLE LEE ADERHOLT
JAMES BRUCE ALFORD
NEIL DAVID BLITZER
JEFFREY BORTNIKER
RAYMOND LEE DRAKE
RONNIE PHILIP CHAPMAN
ROBERT LYNN DAIL
GEORGE DONIGIAN
ROBERT A DURIE
REBECCA ARNETTE HAMPTON
LIGON LOFLIN JONES
PAULA ANNE LEWIS
ELIZABETH HILL PETERSON
WILLIAM LUTHER MITCHELL
PATRICIA ANN PODLEWSKI
CINDY JANE SHUFORD
MARTHA LOUISE SORDELETT
DAVID CRAIG YOUNGBLOOD
WILLIAM COLQUITT GARVIN
BARBARA CATHERINE BUYS
REBECCA SUSAN SWICEGOOD
ROSS FRAZER THORNLEY
GAIL MAGRUDER
TIMOTHY MOORE

1957 TEACHERS

MRS. CHARLOTTE MAGRUDER

MRS. LOUISE PACE

MRS. SUE TRAYLOR

MRS. LYDIA FISHER

PIANISTS: MRS. HEFFINGTON &
MRS. LOUISE PACE

SUBSTITUTE TEACHERS

MRS. BETTY LEWIS   MRS. GEORGE DONIGIAN

Annual Recital

*Students of Thelma Olaker's School of Dance & Mrs. Pace's Students at Hopewell High School, **Saturday May 17, 1958—8 P.M:** Camm Moore, Janie Pritchard, Roma Idell Ameen, Rhonda Cuddihy, Vada Lynn Caricofe, Nancy Jeanne Dougherty, Kathleen Easterling and Billy Traylor; Dee Miller, and Elizabeth Schulhof are not shown. Accompanist for Recital—Lula Cook Wells and Studio Pianist—Joyce E. Reid*

154

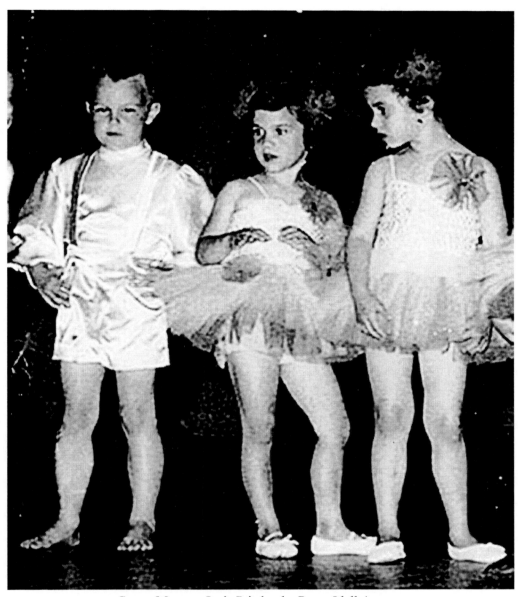

Camm Moore—Janie Pritchard—Roma Idell Ameen,
Jane Claire Pritchard, Henrico Co. Virginia School Teacher

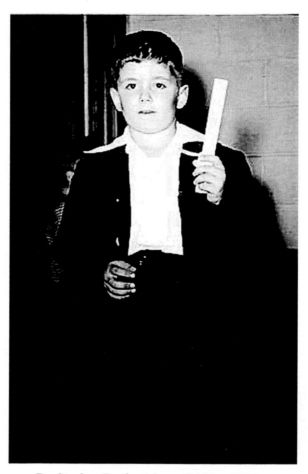

Dr. Stephen Perrine Maxwell MD—1958

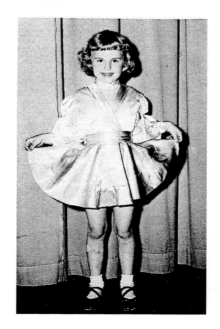

A Dance: "Rock—A Bye Baby" & "Di Diddle Diddle" Dancers:
Janet Deweese, Debbie Cadger, Ann Mabry, Faidra Vasilos, Karen Smith

1958—The Cowboy's, Mrs. Pace is on the Piano: Billy Traylor, Bill Altman, Robert Anderson, Harry Garfinkel, Jimmy Holt, Phillip Maxwell, George Flannagan, Dennis Finn, Jimmy Holt, Steven Garner.

1958—"My Old Staw Hat"
Billy Traylor, Bill Altman, Robert Anderson, , Jimmy Sansing,
Steve Garner, George Flannagan, Jimmy Holt

Mrs. Pace's 2nd & 1st grandchildren;
William Ellsworth Traylor, Jr. Thompson G. Pace III

Left to Right: Mrs. Martha Sue Pace Traylor, Bobby Traylor,
Bill Traylor and Mrs. Pace

Mrs. Pace's 3rd & 2nd grandchildren: Bobby and Billy Traylor

The Hopewell School of Childhood
519 Appomattox Street

1958—School relocated and dramatic play productions briefly were performed on patio. Hopewell, Virginia

Father, taught children how to ride bicycles. He would take off the training wheels; reduce air in the tires, to assist children in their balance.

Mrs. Pace's grandson, William Ellsworth Traylor, Jr.
celebrating his Birthday Party in cuffs.

Mrs. Pace's second grandson William Ellsworth Traylor, Jr.

Hopewell School of Childhood

This Certifies that

WILLIAM EllsworTh TRAylOR JR.

*Having completed the Kindergarten Course of Study is hereby declared
Graduate of the Hopewell School of Childhood and awarded this*

DIPLOMA

Dated, Hopewell, Virginia, _____ May 21 19 58 _____

Sue Pace Traylor Directress

Lannie Pace Teacher

Hopewell School of Childhood

Ninth Annual Commencement

Mrs. Pace's Kindergarten

and Nursery School

Presenting

The Graduating Class of 1958

WEDNESDAY, MAY 21, 1958 ...7:30 P.M.

HOPEWELL HIGH SCHOOL

HOPEWELL VIRGINIA

PROGRAM

SONG …….. "THE CLOCK" …….. By School

WELCOME ………. By Howard Parson

SONGS: "SMILES".."TAKE OFF YOUR WORRY AND PUT
ON A SMILE" and "MOTHER"
(Dedicated by the children to their mothers) By School

GOD BLESS AMERICA ………..

RHYTHM BAND…. Director, Harry Garfinkel
SELECTIONS: "Jingle Bells" "Mocking Bird Hill"
and a "Waltz"

RHYTHM IN PANTONMINE………By Nursery School
Horses…..Butterflies….Skaters….Fishing
Clap—Clap ….My Shadow...March

PLAY …..."THE BALLOON MAN"……
The Balloon Man: Jimmy Sansing,
Karen Smith, Arthur Donigian, Roma Ameen,, Allen Rhyn, Janet
Deweese, Obckie Jerrell, Margaret Neslson, Faidra Vasilos,
William Sterling, Billy Traylor, Jack Aaron, Johnny Hecker

MEXICAN CHIAPANTICS
Rhonda Cuddihy, Roma Ameen, Ann Mabry, Valerie
Kalocokis, Debbie Page, Margaret Ann Nelson, Janet
DeWeese

COWBOY DRILL
BOYS: John Aaron, Bill Altman, Bruce Edwards,
Robert Anderson, George Edwards, George Flannagan,
Harry Garfinkel, Steven Garner, Jimmy Holt, Phillip
Maxwell, Howard Parson, Jonny McBride, George
Wilcox, Billy Traylor, Jonny Hecker, Dennis Finn

A DANCE.."ROCK—A—BYE BABY" & DI DIDDLE DIDDLE
DANCERS: Janet DeWeese, Debbie Cadger, Ann Mabry
Faidra Vasilos, Karen Smith

A PLAY.... "WHEN I GROW UP"

GRANDFATHER: George Wilcox

GRANDMOTHER: Toni Kruzic

GRANDDAUGHTERS: Peggie Jo Pearce, Stephanie Slovic
Debbie Page, Valerie Kalodakis, Linda Woo, Donna Lee

GRANDSONS: Harry Garfinkel, Jonny McBride,
          George Edwards, Bruce Edwards, Dennie Finn

"MY OLD STRAW HAT"

Bill Altman, Robert Anderson, Billy Traylor, Jimmy Sansing,
Steve Garner, George Flannagan, Jimmy Holt

AWARDING OF DIPLOMAS TO—

JOHN LEE AARON
WILLIAM DAVID ALTMAN
ROBERT MAXWELL ANDERSON, III
RHONDA ANN CUDDIHY
BRUCE MARSHALL EDWARDS
GEORGE THOMAS FLANNAGAN
DINNIS FRANCIS FINN
HARRY STEVEN GARFINKEL
STEVEN FORREST GARNER
JOHN ALONZO HECKER
JAMES TYLER HOLT
ROGER IRVING HUGHES
VALERIE KATINA KALODAKIS
ANTONETTE KRUZIC
DONNA MARYE LEE
PHILLIP CONLEE MAXWELL
DEBORAH KAY PAGE
HOWARD TOLAR PARSONS
PEGGY JO PEARCE
JOHN LYTLE McBRIDE, III
STEPHANIE ANDREA SLOVIC
ALIAN DEAN WEISH
GEORGE EDWARD WILLCOX
LINDA WOO
WILLIAM ELLSWORTH TRAYLOR, JR.

SONG .... AMERICA ....BY ALL

TEACHERS

> MRS. LOUISE PACE
> MRS. CHRISTINE MADDY
> MRS. SUE TRAYLOR

SUBSTITUTE TEACHERS

> MRS. NETTIE CARVER
> MRS. MARY HEPLER

Pace's Kindergarten and Nursery School

1959—Teachers: Mrs. Pace and daughter Martha Sue Pace Traylor
Gary Lee Barnes, Ann Cary Bock, Michael Andrew Cadger, Sheila Page Campbell, Barol
Weaver Cofield, Marcie Elizabeth Dail, Marlene Lee De Bault, Susan Page Emory, Eric
Carter Furr, Jo Anne Goodman James Bernard Johnson, Mack Emerald Lewis, Anne Cot-
man Mabry, Caterina Marie Migliardi, Connie Lynn Pentecost, Jane Claire Pritchard,
Karen Margarette Smith, William Ellsworth Traylor, Jr. William John Jaworski, Sandy Lee
Lewis, Sharon Lynn Vance, Daniel Dominic De Mos, Karen Scheirer

HOPEWELL SCHOOL OF CHILDHOOD
TENTH ANNUAL COMMECEMENT

KINDERGARTEN AND NURSERY SCHOOL

Presenting
THE GRADUATING CLASS OF 1959

Friday, May 22, 1959, 6:30 P.M.
"Lawn" at School, 519 Appomattox Street
Hopewell, Virginia

PROGRAM

SONGS: "Vacation is Here"
Good Evening"   By School
WELCOME………………………..   Jimmy Johnson
SONGS: "Good Friends and Neighbors"
"Smiles
"America"…………………….   By School

SONGS: "They Always Pick On Me"….   Billy Traylor
TAP DANCE… "WOODEN SOLDIER"
Eddie Wicker
Wade Rook

RHYTHM BAND   …………   Director, Eric Furr
  SELECTIONS: "Jingle Bells," "Mocking Bird Hill,"
"Dark Town Strutters Ball," Waltz"

DANCE "ROCK—A—BYE BABY" and "HI DIDDLE DIDDLE
  DANCERS: Kathy Seymoure, Debra King, Kriston Scheirer

SONG ……"LITTLE RUBBER COAT"
  RAINCOATS: Arthur Donigian, Ricky Gayhart, Louis
Roeder, Gregory Robertson, Buddy Williams

TAP DANCE…. Steve Mabry and Jackie Wilkerson
DRAMATIZED SONG….THE LITTLE LOST DOG"
         Martha Huntley Sutherland

—CHORUS—

TAMBORINE DANCE…..   **"MEXICAN CHIPANICOS"**
Marlene Debault, Judy Jones,
Debbie Cadger, Carol Cofield,
Sandy Lewis, Karen Scheirer

NURSERY RHYTHM IN PANTOMINE….NURSERY SCHOOL
Horses… Butterflies….Skating…. Clap—Clap—Fishing...
March

BARBERSHOPPERS…..”ON MOONLIGHT BAY”
                      “SIDEWALKS OF NEW YORK”
                      “IN THE GOOD OLD SUMMER TIME”

BOYS: Gary Barnes, Michael Cadger, Eric Furr,
        Jimmy Johnson, Mack Lewis, Donnie DeMos,
        William Jaworski

DANCE ..   “PRETTY BABY”
           Betsy Bonfonti, Sidney Meyers,
           Cheryl Pearson, Mary Lou Wilkerson

BAND…   Nursery Director, Buddy Williams
        SELECTION: “TWINKLE, TWINKLE LITTLE STAR”
        “MARK,” AND “DOGGIE IN THE WINDOW

BUNNIES ON PARADE…Jo Anne Goodman, Ann Bock,
               Marcie Dail, Caterina Migliardi,
               Sharon Vance, Susan Emory, Ann Mabry
               Karen Smith, Connie Pentecost
               Jane Pritchard

SMALL BUNNY ..Sheila Campbell
THE LOAFERS…   Gary Barnes, Michael Cadger,
               Eric Furr, Mack Lewis, William
               Jaworski, Donnie DeMos, Jimmy
               Johnson

DRAMATIZED SONG…   KINDERGARTEN
         “MARY CONTRARY GARDEN”

MARYS	**FLOWERS**
Jane Pritchard	Sheila Campbell
Caterian Migliardi	Karen Smith
Ann Bock	Karen Scheirer
Carol Cofield	Marlene DeBault
Susan Emory	Sharon Vance
Marcie Dail	Jo Anne Goodman
Connie Pentecost	Judy Jones
Anne Mabry	

AWARDING OF DIPLOMAS TO—

GARY LEE BARNES
MICHAEL ANDREW CADGER
SHIELA PAGE CAMPBELL
CAROL WEAVER COFIELD
MARCIE ELIZABETH DAIL
MARLENE LEE DE BAULT
SUSAN PAGE EMORY
ERIC CARTER FURR
JO ANNE GOODMAN
JAMES BERNARD JOHNSON
MACK EMERALD LEWIS
ANNE COTMAN MABRY
CATERINA MARIE MIGLIARDI
CONNIE LYNN PENTECOST
JANE CLAIRE PRITCHARD
KAREN MARGARETTE SMITH
WILLIAM ELLSWORTH TRAYLOR, JR.
WILLIAM JOHN JAWORSKI
SANDY LEE LEWIS
SHARON LYNN VANCE
DANIEL DOMINIC DE MOS
KAREN SCHEIRER

PLEDGE OF ALLEGIANCE……………………..KINDERGARTEN

PRAYER
SONG …….."AMERICA"

TEACHERS

Mrs. Louise Pace
Mrs. Christine Maddy
Mrs. Sue Traylor

SUBSTITUTE TEACHERS
Mrs. Lucille Anderson
Mrs. Bettye Lewis

1960—Mrs. Martha Sue Pace Traylor and Mrs. Eileen Scheirer teacher: Students: Lucy Bowling Anthony, Suzanne Maria Bailey, Mary Elizabeth Booker Arthur Daniel Donigian, Patricia Ann Fager, Benjamin Lee Foley, Joan Beth Goldberg, Geary Steven Hancock, John William Harlan, III, Margarita Maria Laplane, Sydney Allison Myers, Joanne Marie Ortiz, Donna Jean Rigney, Louis Leopold Roeder, Jr., Karen Scheirer, Jay Lester Siagle, William Stephen Slovic, Jr. Margaret Lois Strother, William Jay Traina, III., Gordon Burt Williams, Jr. James Curtis Wright, Jr. Jacqueline Ann Burnham

HOPEWELL SCHOOL OF CHILDHOOD

Dear Patron:

The Hopewell School of Childhood will begin its twelfth session on Monday, September 12, 1960.

This is to advise that I am saving a reservation for your child. If for any reason you will not need the reservation, please advise me promptly by calling GL 8-8257. Patrons are asked to bring their children, complete their enrollment, and visit the schoolroom, Wednesday, August 24 from 10:00 to 12:00 A.M. and from 4:00 to 5:00 P.M. It is requested that all hats, coats, leggings, gloves, galoshes and lunch box or bag be plainly marked with the child's name. This is necessary because very young children do not recognize their possessions among so many similar ones.

Every morning at ten thirty we have our "Tea Party" period. The children bring a very light lunch from home and during this time they are taught table etiquette and social adjustment with a group.

It is possible for your child to bring us a cold as well as get one from contact with us. So, if your child has a cold, please keep him/her at home for 48 hours or until he/she is sufficiently well to be with other children. Should your child be exposed to any of the children's diseases, if you would tell me immediately, I can advise you about the incubation period and when to keep him/her isolated.

If we work together, I feel sure that we will have a happier, healthier group of children.

We will have four parties for the year, Halloween, Christmas, Valentine and Easter.

There will be 36 weeks of school. Holidays to be observed are Thursday and Friday for Thanksgiving, closing December 21 for Christmas, opening on January 3, and Easter Monday—then continuing through May 26, closing of school.

Tuition for Kindergarten and Nursery School is $3.00 per week payable every four weeks in advance as long as enrolled. If more convenient, you may pay the first of each month. Tuition for day nursery will be furnished on request. Transportation will be paid with tuition at $1.50 per week.

I pledge you my loyalty for a happy year with your child and than you for the joyous privilege.

Sincerely Yours,

Louise Pace

(Mrs.) Louise Pace

Tap Dance: Eddie Wicker & Wade Rook—Wooden Soldier

Mrs. Pace and Mrs. Christine Maddy

HOPEWELL SCHOOL OF CHILDHOOD
ELEVENTH ANNUAL COMMENCEMENT

KINDERGARTEN AND NURSERY SCHOOL

Presenting
THE GRADUATING CLASS OF 1960

Friday, May 27, 1960, 7:30 P.M.

"Lawn at School, 519 Appomattox Street

Hopewell, Virginia

******

PROGRAM

VACATION TIME…………………………By School

WELCOME ADDRESS………….……………Lois Strother

WELCOME SONG.. "Take Off Your Worry and Put On a Smile"

 By School

RHYTHM BAND……………………………...By School

Director ……………………………Gordon Williams
Selections:.."Mocking Bird Hill" & Waltz"

RHYTHMS……………………………...Pre—Kindergarten

SONG… "I'm Forever Blowing Bubbles"…………..Eddie Wicker

PLAY………... **"Balloon Man"** ………………………Wade Rook

TAMBORINE DANCE…………………………………………..
Girls: Donna Jean Rigney, Joanne Ortiz, Jackie Burham,
 Mary Booker, Margarita Laplane

DANCE……………………………… "Baa, Baa, Black Sheep"
Ronnie Shaw and Rusty Hughes

DANCE……………………………….. "Pretty Baby"
Kristy Krumel, Deborah Michaelsen, Bobby Traylor, Mariano Betti

SAILERS DRILL…………………………………………………
Jay Slagle Jay Traina
Geary Hancock Louis Roeder
Will Harlan Will Slovic
Arthur Donigian Lee Foley
Gordon Williams Steve Lipscomb

"MAGIC CARPET" ....
>   Susan McBride, Georgie Jenks, Debra King, Mary Sansing,
>   Deborah Michaelsen, Kathy Seymour, Kristen Scheirer,
>   Kristen Krumel, Shelia Roeder

BUNNIES ON PRARADE..
Lucy Anthony, Suzanne Bailey, Mary Booker, Beth Goldberg, Sydney Myers,
Margarita, Laplane, Joanne Ortiz, Donna Jean Rigney, Karen Scheirer, Jackie
Burnham, Nancy Burnham

"HOBO TROUBLE" ....Kindergarten Boys

MUSICAL PLAY ...."When We Grow Up"
Grandmother...Lois Strother
Grandfather..Jay Slagle
Girs..........................Mary Booker, Lucy Anthony,
>   Joanne Ortiz, Beth Goldberg
Boys......................... Steve Lipscomb, James Wright,
>   Gordon Williams, Louis Roeder

DRAMATIZED SONG.. "Umbrella Built for Two" ..Kindergarten
Girls......................Karen Scheirer, Sydney Myers
Boys.....................Steve Lipscomb, James Wright,
>   Gordon Williams, Louis Roeder

"MARY CONTRARY'S GARDEN"...................Kindergarten

MARY'S	**FLOWERS**
Mary Booker	Karen Scheirer
Jackie Burnham	Lucy Anthony
Sydney Myers	Donna Jean Rigney
Louis Strother	Joanne Ortiz
Suzanne Bailey	Janeen Ortiz
Beth Goldberg	Margarita Laplane

AWARDING OF DIPLOMAS TO:

Lucy Bowing Anthony
Suzanne Maria Bailey
Mary Elizabeth Booker
Arthur Daniel Donigian
Patricia Ann Fager
Benjamin Lee Foley
Joan Beth Goldberg
Geary Steven Hancock
John William Harlan, III
Margarita Maria Laplane
Ronald Steven Lipscomb
Sydney Allison Myers
Joanne Marie Ortiz
Donna Jean Rigney
Louis Leopold Roeder, Jr.
Karen Scheirer
Jay Lester Slagle
William Stephen Slovic, Jr.
Margaret Lois Strother
William Jay Traina, III
Gordon Burt Williams, Jr.
James Curtis Wright, Jr.
Jacqueline Ann Burnham

PLEDGE OF ALLEGIANCE………………….....Kindergarten

SONG…………………………………………"America"
TEACHERS

Mrs. Louise Pace
Mrs. Elleen Scheirer
Mrs. Sue Traylor

SUBSTITUTE TEACHERS

Mrs. Frances Johnson
Mrs. Bettye Lewis

MRS. PATRICIA LOUISE ROSS PACE

The founder of the Mrs. Pace's & The Hopewell School of Childhood, and a long time resident of Hopewell, Mrs. Patricia Louise Pace, 72, died at the John Randolph Hospital Saturday, June 10, at 7:45 p.m.

She resided at 519 Appomattox Street and had been ill about two weeks before her death. She was preceded in dead by her husband T. G. Pace Sr., who died in 1947.

A member of the First Methodist church, Mrs. Pace is well known for her active part in the education of children and her interest in their welfare. During World War II, she was instrumental in the schooling of several hundred children of service men.

After founding the Hopewell School of Childhood, Inc. licensed in 1948, she served as its active director and an instructor since that time.

Survivors include a son; T.G. Pace Jr., of Colonial Heights; a daughter, Mrs. William E. Traylor, Sr., of Hopewell and three grandchildren.

Last rites will be held Monday at 2 p.m. in the Chapel of the Gould Funeral Home. The Rev. Walter M. Lockett Jr., pastor of the First Methodist Church, will officiate assisted by the Rev. E. D. Garris, pastor of Highland Methodist Church, Colonial Heights.

Burial will be in Sunset Park Cemetery, Chester.

Chapter 7: Education "Family" Stories

In Grandmother's school, parents, teachers and kids all met on common ground. Parents wanted unparalleled education and peace of mind. Teachers treated caring and learning as inseparable items. The children learned about Hopewell City and the world beyond their environment. It takes a whole community to educate a child.

Mrs. Pace stressed ownership and belonging to create a new and different learning environment. In earnest, she believed that it is not only academic standards in Math, Science, English, History, and Social Studies fields that help young people come out of what we might call deprivation.

Many times, at the end of the school day, an industrial plant employee or construction worker would ask, "Lady what are you teaching my child that they want to live and stay in this school with you all the time?" The children were thankful for all the attention and respect she showed them. There was never a high rate of absenteeism, because the students were excited to be there. Mrs. Pace's school was designed for kid power with an opportunity to grow. The children were the workers and Grandmother was only the manager. Children know when you don't know how to excite them.

When grandmother invited parents to come into her school during the day to observe the classroom activities, they were encouraged not to respond to questions asked by the teachers to the children. The parents impatiently sat and wished to answer the questions for their children. The students would sit back and watch their parents stressed reactions, wondering if this was what learning is all about.

Grandmother saw study in the arts as an essential means---not an end---to acquiring thinking skills, creativity, the ability to change, and the facility to teach oneself. In a safe, nurturing environment, the arts enable students to express their feelings, communicate thoughts, explore their creativity, solve problems, communicate ideas, develop a sense of community, and appreciate themselves as participants in history, tradition, and culture. Learning in art, dance, drama, film, and music advances and strengthens motor skills, promotes considerate behavior, ability to work well with others, self-discipline, perception, and sensitivity. Fine Arts experiences contribute to the developmental process of understanding one another and naturally motivate students in all their learning.

Dance - Kindergarten

"Children have a natural instinct to move - to jump or leap for joy, roll with laughter, melt with disappointment, or contract with fear. Movement helps them master their world and determine who they are. Their intuitive responses and explorations of movement become the material of the elementary dance core curriculum. Through this curriculum, students transform everyday movement into dance by focusing on the sensory experience They learn to value themselves and others as unique individuals with the ability to move, create, and respond to ideas, concepts, feelings, and relationships through dance. Children discover that, as unique and creative human beings, the power to find joy and personal connections resides within themselves."

Music - Kindergarten

"Music is the natural extension of the human heartbeat. Emotions are brought to the surface and melted together with thought by its imaginative rhythms and patterns of sound. It makes work and play more enjoyable and provides a way for children to relate to and express their feelings about the events of the day, their friends and family, differences in people, and the mechanical and natural wonders of the world about them. Singing, playing, exploring, creating, and listening to music will help them to recognize and describe its elements, discover its messages, increase their perception of sound, and invent their own musical expressions. They will also gain skills in working together, solving problems, thinking analytically and connecting with other subjects they are learning."

Theatre - Kindergarten

"The Drama Core builds a bridge between play and learning. In the years before kindergarten, when blankets were thrown over tables became dangerous caves and parents' old clothes grew into brave, new explorers, playing at drama taught us about being human. Beginning with kindergarten, the drama core helps us learn how to work together when we are people in a place with a problem to solve. Walking in the shoes of others helps us understand others and participate successfully in the making of a neighborhood, be it of people next door or people around the world."

Visual Arts - Kindergarten

"The Visual Arts disciplines students to take greater meaning and a refined sense of beauty from the world that surrounds them. The Visual Arts give them practice in decoding the worlds of the past as well as a deeper understanding of and ability to cope with our visual culture with its nonstop parade of images and enticements. The Visual Arts give students time to interpret their own lives and to create objects that carry meaning important to them individually as well as to their generation. It gives them a means to analyze and plan."

From A Mothers' Job: The History of Daycare, 1890-1960 by Elizabeth Rose, Oxford University Press, Inc., 1999

Grandmother, the character, the artist, and the musician wrote the words, music and played piano for all her productions. Here are a selected number of unpublished songs. Many songs were lost to a large flood in 1988.

Welcome Song— Take off Your Troubles and Put on a Smile –
Good Friends & Neighbors

We Hope You've Brought Your Smiles Along

Pal of My School Days Come Back To Me.

We're Mighty Glad You Came

Baby Talk

PAL OF MY SCHOOL DAYS
COME BACK TO ME.

185

LASS PLEASE COME BACK TO ME BRING THE VI-SION I FAILED TO
VID-ED THE OLD PATH-WAY BUT THOUGHTS OF THE PAST WILL COME AND

REFRAIN

SEE;
STAY;

PAL OF MY

P-MF

WORDS OF RE-GRET I NOW BRING TO YOU, TELL-ING EACH TRUTH TO

ALL THE FLOW'RS, TIME CAN-NOT RE-PLACE THOSE GOLD-EN HOURS,

186

Chapter 8 Neighborhoods

The young people were given back the childhood they may never have had. The children were taught something they could use later in life. I learned from a powerful education mentor, Dr. William C. Bosher Jr., former Virginia State Superintendent, Dean of the School of Education at Virginia Commonwealth University, that creativity and imagination are the most "sophisticated chalkboards" we've ever known.

It is hard work that determines success, not ability. The best teacher is the one who suggests rather then dogmatizes, and inspires his or her listener with the wish to teach themselves.

Grandmother was so far ahead of many educators in her methodology of creative adaptation, because she wanted new ideas. Our world is so immediate today. There is so much out there we can tap into. We need to bridge beyond the immediate into actuality-reality. Some teachers teach irrelevant studies. In Grandmother's school the older children helped assist the younger ones, like a sister or brother. Again, it was <u>family.</u>

She had a minimum of discipline problems. Her school was a laboratory, a school-testing environment with new ways to teach, innovating new teaching concepts, but always operating under state and city regulations and guidelines. Her code of ethics was to never do anything to the children in her hands that she would not do to her own biological child.

Teachers Deserving Of More Respect

The school year is in full swing, and I remember the days when I was in grade school. Life was so simple for me back in the late 1950's and early to late 60's.

Junior high came and went, and then it was on to high school. I have fond memories of the teachers who were tireless in their devotion to helping me learn. And I salute their efforts in teaching me and the many young minds before and after me. Fast-forward to 2014, and the picture looks a lot different. In some areas, it looks downright grim. I am referring to the lack of respect and the tumultuous environments that some of the nation's teachers endure throughout the school year.

I would post it that our K-12 educational system is somewhat under siege. In what parallel universe is it OK to swear at your teacher, berate your teacher, make fun of your teacher and, in some cases, inflict bodily harm on your teacher? I have been told that some children tear up their papers and throw them in the trash, saying I'm not going to do it.

Having been brought up in the Methodist faith, I can recall my father telling me about his experience in parochial schools. I find it interesting hearing about the teachers and the strict policies that were in place when my dad was growing up. You might say good old Dr. Spock might take issue with the teachers' tactics with regard to discipline.

I remember hearing about the occasional whack on the knuckles if one spoke out of turn or dared to "act out" in class. I looked at my father's hands and I didn't see any battle scars form the proverbial ruler that the teachers may have used, but I did see a set of hands that exhibited an enduring work ethic, strength, character and, above all discipline.

Whoever rears us must teach us that discipline along the way. Teachers can certainly model positive behavior and be guiding lights to young, impressionable minds, but it is incumbent upon the caregiver to teach the child to respect authority, in this case the teacher.

We've all had teachers we loved and others we didn't, but it is never OK to bully a teacher. Moreover, safeguards need be in place to make the classroom a beacon of hope and encouragement for the next generation.

Teachers cannot teach in a chaotic environment where they fear for the worst, nor can anyone prosper in a learning environment fraught with disrespect.

I have a daughter, Loraine Wesler and close friends who are teachers; one is Lorie Preston, a Para-Professional teacher for Special Education Students in Powhatan, Virginia. She is a great story teller, like her father, my friend, Tom Kagel. The children in her classroom the moment she enters begin to cry, not in fear of physical discipline, but strict dedicated hard work lessons expected from them to demonstrate their talents.

In current education, many teachers are excellent, but they rarely have the opportunity to demonstrate how good they are because so much of classroom time is wasted handling disciplinary problems. I see teachers in tears because of the treatment they receive from students trying to show off for others. Things almost turn violent when a substitute is unfortunate enough to be cast into the "den of lions."

During the life of Mrs. Pace's school, the parents who couldn't afford to pay an hour or day's tuition were given alternate special payment plans that continued till the closing of the school in 1986. Many parents shared personal heartfelt stories in not having enough money to pay for daycare. Most of them only made one hundred dollars or less a month.

Grandmother and Mother never pressured, refused, nor deprived any parent for child care services. In providing this type of child care service it reflected today's education standard, **"No Child Left Behind."** No child ever suffered or was excluded nor neglected. Children have always been innocent from society's cultural economic hardships.

Communication with parents was the most challenging. A majority of the parents were working low-income families. Other educational daycare centers originating later did not encourage parents to participate in classroom school events or to view behaviors they saw when they dropped off their children. Grandmother had the solution. When parents had the chance to observe their children playing they were amazed that Mrs. Pace's was a safe place for their children. They became believers and active supporters of Mrs. Pace's school and realized these were not just ordinary educators, teachers, but special people who destroyed limitations. Her philosophy and programs encouraged the children to be on fire and have a love for learning.

189

In college I had the opportunity to recite poetry or dramatic prose before an audience who rated them in terms of style and effectiveness. There I acquired a great deal of confidence in my ability to speak in public. The vast majority of teachers not only pour themselves tirelessly into their work for the sake of their students, they also forgo all kinds of recognition and financial compensation to do so.

Little Bo Peep—Tamera Joyner   Little Boy Blue—Michael Stout

1961—RIDE-A-COCK-HORSE

Frederic Birchett, Michael Thornton, Wayne Pentecost, Sidney Hudson, Edward Wicker, Larry Hildebrand, Rickie Campbell, John Kippy Causey, Barry Wyatt, Robert Gill, Michael B. Alexandra, Michael Stout

1961—MARY CONTRARY'S GARDEN (FLOWERS)

Georgia Jenks, Shelia Roeder, Christie Aderholt, Susan McBride Virginia Foster, Debra King, Tamara Joyner, Kristie, Krumel Cheryl Pearson, and Susan Garfinkel

Umbrella Built For Two-1961

1961 Nursery: Bobby Traylor, Kristie Krumel, Eddie Wicker, Shelia Roeder, Ronnie Shaw.

1961—Mrs. Pace's third grandson, Robert Pace Traylor

HOPEWELL SCHOOL OF CHILDHOOD

TWELTH ANNUAL COMMENCEMENT

KINDERGARTEN AND NURSERY SCHOOL

Presenting

THE GRADUATING CLASS OF 1961

Wednesday, May 24, 1961, 8:00 P.M.

"Lawn" at school

519 Appomattox Street

Hopewell, Virginia

PROGRAM

SONGS: "Vacation Days".........................By School

     "God Bless Americaa.......................School

WELCOME........................Michael Bruce Alexandri

SONGS: "Smiles...............................By School

     "Good Friends and Neighbors"

PLAY........... **"FAIRY FUN"** .... Nursery School

Fairies	Elves
Nancy Burnham	Spotswood Bowyer
Jayne Woolridge	Maro Lebow
Jan Woolridge	Mark Latino
Jane Wall	Randy Mays
Rhonda Wells	Rusty Hughes
	Tommy Bell
Queen	C. I. Smith
Nancy Locicero	Randy Birchett
	Kenny Moffitt
	Ronnie Shaw

RIDE—A—COCK—HORSE	HANSEL AND GRETEL DANCE
Frederic Birchett	
Michael Thornton	**Hansel's**
Wayne Pentecost	Milton Myers
Sidney Hudson	Hardy King
Edward Wicker	Michael Stout
Larry Hildebrand	Frederick Mecker
Rickie Campball	John Chezik
John Kippy Causey	
Barry Wyatt	**Gretel's**
Robert Gill	Joyce Lee
Michael B. Alexandri	Tamara Joyner
Michael Stout	Patti Page
	Elizabeth Traina
	Tracy Sutton

MARY CONTRARY'S GARDEN (Flowers)

Georgia Jenks	Susan McBride
Shelia Roeder	Virginia Foster
Christie Aderholt	

MARYS

Debra King   Cheryl Pearson

Tamera Joyner   Susan Garfinkel

Kristie Krummel

THE MOTHER GOOSE PARTY

Cast, in order of appearance

Old King Cole............................Frederic Birchett

1st Fiddler................................Edward Wicker

2nd Fiddler...............................Milton Myers

3rd Fiddler...............................Barry Wyatt

Curley Locks.............................Joyce Lee

Little Boy Blue...........................Michael Stout

Little Bo Peep...........................Tamara Joyner

Little Jack Horner......................John Kippy Causey

Jack......................................Larry Hildebrand

Jill.......................................Debra King

Butcher..................................Sidney Hudson

Baker....................................Wayne Pentecost

Candlestick Maker......................Michael Thornton

Little Miss Muffet......................Susan McBride

Mary......................................Christie Aderholt

Simple Simon............................Hardy King

Pieman...................................Frederick Hecker

Peter.....................................Rickie Campbell

Jack Spratt...............................Robert Gill

His Wife..................................Tracy Sutton

Queen of Hearts..........................Cheryl Pearson

Little Girl With Curl.....................Patti Page

Humpty Dumpty.........................John Chezik

Polly.....................................Georgia Jenks

Suky.....................................Kristie Krumel

Pease Porridge Hot.......................Susan Garfinkel

Pease Porridge Cold.....................Shelia Roeder

Little Tommy Tucker....................Michael Alexandri

Old Woman in the Shoe.................Virginia Foster

AWARDING OF DIPLOMAS

PLEADGE OF ALLEGIANCE

SONG............................AMERICA

TEACHERS

Mrs. Louise Pace - Mrs. Carol Flack - Mrs. Sue Traylor

PIANIST   Mrs. Charles Skinner

198

*1962—Theodora Penelope Andrew, Holly Preston Harrison, Mary Ellen Holt, Nancy Karen Locicero, Mary Katherine Moore, Debra Susan Rigney, Kireten Scheirer, Shirley Ann Schneider, Pamela Maus Seavy, Margaret Elizabeth Taylor, Suzanne Ulmer, Mairle Day Wright, James Thomas Bell, Randolph Gay Birchett, John Spotswood Bowyer, Alvin Zack Cox, III, Michael Edward Crupenink, Loren Douglas Dillingham, Paul Eric Enclinas, William Ford Flannagan, Jay Walter Gould, Edward Page Henry, III, Gary Brick Humphrey, William Calvin King, Mark Anthony Latino, James Louis Schulhof, Ronald Elwood Shaw, James Albert Simons, Fred Kirkpatrick Youngblood, **Mrs. Carl Flack, Teacher***

HOPEWELL SCHOOL OF CHILDHOOD

THIRTEENTH ANNUAL COMMENCEMENT

KINDERGARTEN

Presenting

THE GRADUATING CLASS OF 1962

Wednesday, May 23, 1962, 7:30 P.M.

Patrick Copeland School

Hopewell, Virginia

PROGRAM

THE LITTLE DUTCH KINDERGARTEN

Introduction:	Mary Katherine Moore
Dutch Mother and Father	Suzanne Ulmer
	Douglas Dillingham

HANSEL AND GRETEL DANCERS

Suzanne Ulmer	Douglas Dillingham
Mary Katherine Moore	Calvin King
Pamela Seavy	Ronald Shaw
Holly Harrison	Gary Humphrey
Shirley Schneider	Fred Youngblood
Penny Andrew	Edward Henry

TULIPS

Nancy locicero	Kirsten Scheirer

DAFFODILS

Mairie Wright	Mary Ellen Holt	Debra Rigney

DAISY AND ROBIN

Betsy Taylor	Randy Birchett

MARY CONTRARY'S GARDEN

Suzanne Ulmer	Betsy Taylor
Mary Katherine Moore	Mary Ellen Holt
Pamela Seavy	Mairie Wright
Holly Harrison	Debra Rigney
Shirley Scheider	Nancy Locicero
Penny Andrew	Kirsten Scheirer

THE LAND OF THE DUTCH

Jay Gould	Mark Latino
Michael Cruppenink	Jimmy Simon
Tommy Bell	Paul Encinas
Zack Cox	James Schuihof

WYNKEN, BLYNKEN AND NOD

AWARDING OF DIPLOMAS

Theodora Penelope Andrew
Holly preston Harrison
Mary Ellen Holt
Nancy Karen Locicero
Mary Katherine Moore
Debra Susan Rigney
Kirsten Scheirer
Shirley ann Achneider
Pamela Maus Seavy
Margaret Elizabeth Taylor
Suzanne Ulmer
Mairle Day Wright
James Thomas Bell
Randolph Gay Birchett
John Spotswood Bowyer
Alvin Zack Cox, III
Michael Edward Cruppenink
Loren Douglas Dillingham
Paul Eric Encinas
William Ford Flannagan
Jay Walter Gould
Edward Page Henry, III
Gary Brick Humphrey
William Calvin King
Mark Anthony Latino

James Louis Schuihof
Ronald Elwood Shaw
James Albert Simons
Fred Kirkpatrick Youngblood

THE PLEDGE OF ALLEGIANCE TO THE FLAG

DIRECTORESS: Mrs. William E. Traylor

TEACHER: Mrs. Donald R. Flack

PIANIST: Mrs. Ivan Christoffell

1963—Old King Cole, C.I. Smith; 1st Fiddler; Tripp Wilson;
2nd Fiddler; Denny Andrew; 3rd Fiddler; Charles Booker;

Little Miss Muffet, Laura McBride; Spider, Glenn Hughes;

1963—Kathy Blanchard, Patricia Coury, Pat Henerson, Laura McBride, JoAnn Perez, Patti Pritchard, Betty Seavy, Constance Warren, Rhonda Watson, Rhonda Wells, Jan Woolridge, Jayne Woolridge, Stewart Almond, Dean Andrews, Billy Bellefontaine, Charles Booker, Gregory Campbell, Gary Edwards, Robert Gessell, Dan Harlan, Glenn Hughes, Jay Leadbetter, David Martin, Randall Mays, Bennie Miller, James Savage, C.I. Smith, Roy Tatum, Dean Andrews, Diane Latino, Billy Michaels, Sarah Stout, Tripp Wilson, Patsy Hatch, Patty Simmons, Donnie Wells, Bell Jerry, Karen Stevens and Jackie Cleeve.

Dr. Dean Andrews M.D.—Physician
Rhonda Watson B.S., M. Ed.—Teacher
Patti Pritchard—Attorney-At-Law: College of William & Mary
Stewart Almond—Financial Consultant

LINED UP HERE on stage at Patrick Copeland is the graduating class at the Hopewell School of Childhood. Diplomas earned this year were presented.

(Fred Phillips Photo)

204

1963—Jayne & Jan Woodridge

1963—End Of Year Event

School Of Childhood Graduates Group At

Commencement Program.

A program, **"Mother Goose Mischief Makers,"** and presentation of diplomas marked the closing exercises for the Hopewell School of Childhood on Appomattox Street.

For the fourteenth annual commencement for the kindergarten and nursery directed by Mrs. William E. Traylor, the program was held in the auditorium at Patrick Copeland School.

Mrs. Traylor was assisted by Mrs. Donald Flack teacher; Mrs. Ivan Christoffel, pianist; David Merricks and David Flack, set: and Mrs. Allen Flannagan, coordinator.

Members of the cast were:

Old Woman in the Shoe, Jo An Perex; Old King Cole, C.I. Smith; 1st Fiddler; Tripp Wilson; 2nd Fiddler; Deanie Andrew; 3rd Fiddler; Charles Booker; Curley Locks, Connie Warren; Little Boy Blue, Stewart Almond; Little Bo Peep, Pat Henderson; Little Miss Muffet, Laura McBride; Spider, Glenn Hughes; Humpty Dumpty, Jimmy Savage; Pease Porridge Hot, Betty Seavy; Pease Porridge Cold, Pattie Pritchard; Polly, Jayne Woolridge; Suky, Jan Woolridge; Little Jack Horner, Randy Mays; Jack, Dan Harlan; Jill, Kathy Blanchard; Baker, David Martin; Candlestick Maker, Robbie Gessell; Butcher, Jay Leadbetter; Mary, Patricia Coury;

Jack Be Nimble, Bennie Miller; Peter, Gregory Campbell; Peter's Wife, Ann Bolger; Girl with a Curl, Rhonda Lynn Watson; Mistress Mary Rhonda Sue Wells; Wynken, Gary Edwards; Blyken, Scott Hancock; Nod, Billy Bellefontaine; and Puff, Jimmy Savage.

Graduates" who received diplomas were:

Kathy Sue Blanchard, Ann Marie Bolger, Patricia Coury, Patricia Ann Henderson, Laura Ellis McBride, Jo Ann Perez, Patricia Lettie Pritchard, Elizabeth Eaton Seavy, Constance Sue Warren, Rhonda Lynn Watson, Rhonda Sue Wells, Jan Woolridge, Jayne Woolridge, William Stewart Almond IV., Constantine Theodore Andrew, Billy Bellefontaine, Charles Woodson Booker, Gregory Lee Campbell, Gary Wayne Edwards, Robert Gessell, Scott Thomas Hancock, Dan Harlan, Glenn Hughes, James Lawson Leadbetter, David Preston Martin, Jr., Randall Goodwin Mays, George Benjamin Miller Jr., James Nelson Savage, Clarence Ivey Smith III., Norwood Williams Wilson., III

——————— *end of Hopewell News article* ———————

1963—Nancy Burnham, Jane Wall, Patricia Pritchard,
Jayne & Jan Woodridge, Rhonda Wells

208

Virginia (Diddy) Ford Flannagan, was Martha Sue Pace Traylor's life-long friend, companion, neighbor and devoted infamous kindergarten teacher for seventeen years. Mrs. Flannagan scripted playbills, choreographed dramatic plays and as grandmother, made costumes for all mother's students.

(Diddy) Flannagan graduated Hopewell High School in 1943, attended Longwood College and transferred to The University of Virginia to finish her Bachelors of Arts Teachers degree.

Mother's dear and close friend, Virginia (Diddie) Flannagan, shared many wonderful stories with me about how she and Mother wrote their humorous children's play stories and scripts late at night in the kitchen cooking lasagna or meatloaf and having a couple glasses of wine.

Mrs. Flannagan told me a story one day about a students comment on their coats being turned inside out. She said, "she would spend half the afternoon turning the children's coats back correctly." We all know the old saying that, out of the mouths of babes come revelations. This was one of those times. Because, one day a child asked Diddy, Mrs. Flannagan, why are you turning our coats back, they will be OK when we go home." Just then the young man placed his arms in the coat to reverse.

Here is one of their dramatic plays: **"The Shoemaker's Tea Party"** This dramatic Play was written by Mrs. Flannagan and Mother.

Script: Shoemaker:
Curtain opens and all stand say pledge of allegiance.

Shoemaker: I live in a house in the woods.
I never have time to play.
I'm the cobbler—I make the shoes.
I have to work all day.

Shoemaker: You've made me as happy as can be, won't you sing some more for me?

Mary: While you're working on my shoe— I can sing a song for you
Sings: Mary Had a little Lamb.
All sing— Mary walks around with lamb—curties and sits.

Polly: You've got the blues—-that's for sure.
We have got the perfect cure!

Suky: We're having a party—you come, too
We'll sing a song just for you!

Curtain opens—children seated around shop all sing Wee Little Man.

Baa Baa Black Sheep:
Shoemaker: You've brought me some wool, what a nice thing to do.
Baa Baa: I am very nice, but this is not for you.

Deedle Deedle Dumpling—
I think I'm going out of my head, my little boy wears one shoe to bed.

Humpty Dumpty: I can sing very well
Shoemaker: Be careful not to crack your shell!
H.D. falls off wall

Little Miss Muffet: I bought these shoes but something wrong.
Shoemaker: I can fix them—Sing your song!
Sings: Little Miss Muffet—Along comes the spider.
Spider comes out Miss Muffet runs to chair Curties and sits.

Spider: Something's not right, I can't eat!
Shoemaker: You've just got too many feet!
Sings: Eensy Weensy Spider.

6 Little Ducks
Shoemaker: I can't do a thing for you! Who ever saw a duck with a shoe?
Sings: Six Little Ducks.

Farmer:
Shoemaker: Hello, Mr. Farmer—are you all right?
Did you tell your family to stay at home tonight?
Wife, child, nurse, dog, cat, rat, and cheese.

Little Boy Blue, brings shoe to Shoemaker: Sing Little Boy Blue.
Oh, my! Oh, my! Where are my sheep?
Shoemaker: They all ran away, while you were asleep!
Blew horn!

Indian: We'll do a dance if you will, too?
Shoemaker: There's nothing I would rather do.

Petunia
Shoemaker: This Flower is pretty (holds Petunia) but this doesn't match (holds onion)
All sing "Lonely Little Petunia." Petunia Stands and Cries—Bows & Sits

Muffin Man: I'd pass my cakes—but there's a nail in my shoe.
Shoemaker: I can get it out for you!
Sings: Muffin Man

Mr. and Mrs. Pumpkin:
Mr. Pumpkin: I found this pretty shell for you— If I stay here—you do too.
Sing: "Peter Peter Pumpkin Eater."
Peter chases Ms. Pumpkin around the shell—puts her in—she pulls him in too.

Mary Contrary:
Mary: You're standing where my flowers should be.
Shoemaker: There's nothing here that I can see!

Mary: I could have planted them a little deep, but if you don't move, I'll water your feet!
Sings: Mary Contrary Garden

Jack Be Nimble: I can jump and I can sing!
Shoemaker: Go ahead—Do your thing!
Sings: Jack Be Nimble

Little Bow Peep: My sheep have gone they're really bad!
Shoemaker: Sing you song—Don't be sad
Sings: Little Bow Peep

Jack and Jill:
Shoemaker: My pail is empty, as you can see—will someone get some water for me?
Jack and Jill takes the pail and sings Jack and Jill.

Twinkle Star:
Twinkle Star: That light up there is as small as a pin. I wonder where they plug it in?
Shoemaker: There's no cord to go that far, that little light is called a star!
Sings: Twinkle Twinkle Little Star.

Suky: We're all as tired as can be,

Let's all stop and have some tea!

Polly: I have a very pretty pot.
Let's all drink it while it's hot!

Sing Polly Put the Kettle On.

Shoemaker: I've had a good time – you've all been funny.
Now, I'd like to have some money. Pass the Piggy bank.
Your shoes are fixed –you paid your fee.
You've all been very nice to me.
There's one more thing I'd like to do.
I'd like to teach a song to you.
Sing: **"I'd like to teach the World to Sing."**

Class Program:
" The Shoemaker's Tea Party"

	CAST
Shoemaker:	Scott Barnes
Polly:	Jessica Palmer
Suky:	Caroline York
Mary:	Mary Childs
Yankee Doodle:	Wayne Peppers
Humpty Dumpty:	Patrick Spacek

6 Little Ducks:	Aaron Dereski
	Jeanne Chow
	Christina Spacek
	Jason Case
	Vincent Manieri
	Jenny Reynolds
	Ruth Harris
	Mandy Sublette
Farmer:	Todd Convington
Farmer's Wife:	Jenny Reynolds
Child:	Trey Montogomery
Nurse:	Muriel Caton
Dog:	Billy Ellis
Cat:	Chris Keemer
Rat:	Eddie Price
Cheese:	Vincent Manieri
Miss Muffet:	Jennifer Lipscomb
Spider:	Fred Wawner
Boy Blue:	Randy Minter
Indian:	Zachery Hess
Muffin Man:	David Carpenter
Mr. Pumpkin:	Joseph Wagner
Mrs. Pumpkin:	Paige Wagner
Bow Peep:	Billie Jo Davis
Jack Be Nimble:	Kevin Morris
Mary Contrary:	Stacie Pardew
Jack:	Aaron Dereski
Jill:	Christy Gerhart
Petunia:	Anna Marie Downing

Snow White—enters from center
7 Dwarves—from each side

Karen	**Snow White**	Come little friends listen to me We're going to have Some company. Mother Goose & Her children are coming to see why the Prince hasn't come to marry me.
Chris	**Dwarf # 1**	He should have come long ago we have looked high and low.
Tommy	**Dwarf # 2**	He will come most any day.
Gregg	**Dwarf # 3**	Unless, of course, he lost his way.
Stephen	**Dwarf # 4**	He may have married another instead or maybe a dragon killed him dead.
Karen	**Snow White**	Oh, come now, don't be pests!
Scott L.	**Dwarf # 5**	Let's hurry home and greet our guest.

Curtains open—Mother Goose & Children have arrived and
are busily looking around.

Morgan	**Mother Goose**	Where's the Prince? We've looked everywhere! And where's your castle in the air?
Joel	**Dwarf # 6**	We wish he'd come He's very late Our house is much too small for eight.
Karen	**Snow White**	He really is inclined to tarry I'll find someone else to marry!
Stephanie		Jill pulls Jack to center stage—both carry pail.
Deno	**Jill**	I'd gladly let you marry Jack But this pail will break my back!

Jack & Jill sing "Jack & Jill"

All sing while Jack & Jill run up hill and fall down.
Jack help Jill up. Both bow & sit.

214

Michael	**Peter**	I'd marry you in a minute
		But your shell has someone in it!

Peter & Wife sing   "Peter Pumpkin Eater"
All sing. Peter & Wife bow & site.

Jena	**Miss Muffet**	I hope there's a wedding
		I really do
		For a gift, I'll give my spider to you!

Spider	Sings "Little Miss Muffett"

All sing **"Little Miss Muffett"** - Bows & Sits
All sing Encie Weencie Spider

Cynthia   Peas Porridge Hot– He's bound to be late—All boys are the same.

Pamela   Peas Porridge Cold—While we're waiting lets play a game.
Wanda   Peas Porridge Hot & Peas Porridge Cold bow & Sit.

Teresa   All do it facing front—Hot & Cold bow & Sit.

John	**Humpty Dumpty**	I'll take a look from my wall
		I don't think he's coming at all.

FALLS

Humpty Dumpty sings "Humpty Dumpty"
All sing "Humpty Dumpty" bows & sits on floor by wall.

Bruce   **Farmer** (Gets up with hoe(While I'm here
                I'll plant some flowers
                They'll be blooming in 2 hours!

Sings "Farmer in the Dell"

All sing while farmer plants flowers. Farmer bows & sits.

Flowers take places—Mary brings watering cans.

Mary Contrary Dance

Meriwether—**Suky**   Now lets all have a cup of tea.
        Polly & Suky sing "Polly Put the Kettle On"
        All sing "Poly & Suky bow & sit.

215

Betsy	**Mary**	My lamb and I will look and see
		If there's a Prince behind a tree.

Mary sings "Mary and Little Lamb"

All sing—   Mary bows & sits.

Scott M	**Boy Blue**	
		I'd marry her if she knew how
		to keep up with my sheep & cow.

Boy Blue sings "Little Boy Blue"

All   sing while he blows horn—bows & sits.

Manya	**Bow Peep**	He may have tarried along the way
		and like my sheep, has gone astray.

Bow Peep sings "Little Bow Peep: - all sing while she
                    looks for sheep—bow & sit.

Richard **3 Men in Tub**	1st—We're always together as you see.
Stan	2nd—We'd like to have you company.
Mark M.	3rd—But there is only room for three.

     All   We're all as sorry as can be.

Mother Goose   There must be a way to lend the Prince speed.
                A good search party is what we need.
                If there were Indians here about
                I'm sure that they could rout him out.

Mike	**Indian Chief**	Good Lady, here we are at hand
		Your slightest wish is our command!

Tamara **Girl with lost dog**	I sent my dog to look around.
	Your Prince is nowhere to be found.
	And now my dog has lost his way,
	He hasn't been at home all day.

     Sings "Oh Where Oh Where"
     All sing while she looks around—bows & sits.

Humpty Dumpty   The Prince is coming
                I can see from my wall—Point right

Mother Goose   There'll be a wedding after all!

                Takes veil from suitcase—puts it on Snow White

Witch enters from left with apple.
Witch: Here's the apple for Snow White
                She should only take one bite.

Mother Goose	Take your apple and go away
	We haven't got time to do it that way.
Snow White	The Prince is coming as you can see
	And apples don't agree with me.

Witch—shrugs and walks off eating apple.

Mother Goose   (to the Audience) We've made a few changes
We hope you don't mind
We thank you for being
Exceedingly Kind!

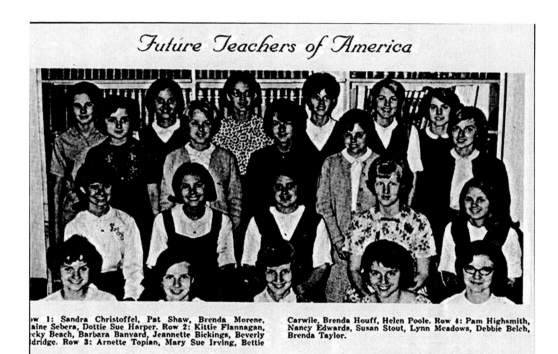

Future Teachers of America

Row 1: Sandra Christoffel, Pat Shaw, Brenda Morene, Elaine Sebera, Dottie Sue Harper.
Row 2: Kittie Flannagan—daughter of Mother's close friend and kindergarten teacher,
Becky Beach, Barbara Banvard, Jeannette Bickings, Beverly Aldridge. Row 3: Arnette To-
pian, Mary Sue Irving, Bettie Carwile, Brenda Houff, Helen Poole. Row 4: Pam Highsmith,
Nancy Edwards, Susan Stout, Lynn Meadows, Debbie Belch, Brenda Taylor.

1964—Graduates of the Hopewell School of Childhood were awarded diplomas at the 19th Annual Commencement exercises.

Sarah Stout, Mark Warner, Michael Miller, Judith Chezik, Diane Latino, Margaret Goldberg, Vickie Watson, Darrel Garner, James Gooman, Douglas Wyatt, Stephan Bellflowers, James Parsons, Barbara Doulis, Mary Agnes Rohlic, Donna Carrel, Gary Lee Blanchard, Billy Michaels, Gary Slagle, Barbara Booker, Gordon McDiarmid, Rebecca Bowyer, Keith Roman, Simons Patricia, Roy Tatum, Patricia Hatch, Johncie Flannagan, Ronald Bell, Barbara Butterworth, Michael O'Conner, Ronald Rogers, James Elliott, Kathleen Bellefontaine, Frances Nesbett, Ray Garfinkel, Peter Lorenzen, William Henry, Ann Easterling, and Sam Rafey.

1964 Hopewell School of Childhood Kindergarten Report Card

READINESS

S	S
I	S
S	S
S	S
S	E
E	L
E	L

- PARTICIPATES IN CONVERSATION.
- PAYS ATTENTION WHEN OTHERS ARE TALKING.
- ENJOYS LISTENING TO STORIES AND POEMS.
- SHOWS AN INTEREST IN PICTURE AND STORY BOOKS.
- SPEAKS CLEARLY AND DISTINCTLY.
- EXPRESSES HIS IDEAS AND EXPERIENCES WELL.
- SHOWS INTEREST IN WORDS, NUMBERS AND COLORS.

HEALTH AND SAFETY

S	S
L	E
L	E
S	S
I	S
S	S

- RELAXES AND RESTS QUIETLY.
- KNOWS HIS NAME AND ADDRESS.
- KNOWS HIS PHONE NUMBER.
- OBEYS SCHOOL SAFETY RULES.
- IS CAREFUL NOT TO HURT OTHERS.
- RECOGNIZES FAMILIAR LANDMARKS OF LOCALE.

WORK HABITS

E	E
	S
	E
	S
	S

- FOLLOWS DIRECTIONS.
- WORKS WELL WITH THE OTHER CHILDREN.
- PLANS AND FINISHES HIS WORK.
- CLEANS UP PROPERLY.
- USES MATERIALS WELL AND WISELY.

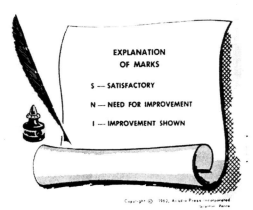

SOCIAL HABITS

S	S
S	S
S	S
S	S
S	S
S	S

- COOPERATES WITH THE TEACHER AND OTHER CHILDREN.
- GETS ALONG WELL WITH OTHER CHILDREN.
- SHOWS HE IS DEVELOPING GOOD MANNERS.
- IS REASONABLY QUIET IN ROOM AND HALLS.
- RESPECTS RIGHTS AND PROPERTIES OF OTHERS.
- MAKES GOOD USE OF HIS TIME IN FREE ACTIVITY.

TO THE PARENT—— OUR PARTNER:

May we work together in a common interest--that of our children.

Through this progress report we present you with a picture of your child's social habits and capabilities as well as his progress in the subject matter areas.

We wish to call to your attention the fact that no two individuals are alike in all respects, and we must be conscious of this at all times. Please do not, therefore, compare your child with other children but measure him according to his ability.

If your child does things successfully, commend him. If his progress report indicates that he needs additional help, do not reprimand him but better, come to the school for a conference where his problems may be discussed with the one who knows most about his social and his work habits--the teacher.

Many hours are devoted to knowing your child better during the time he spends in our schools. And we want you to know, that no opportunity is ever lost in the development of your child's personality along happy and wholesome channels.

With your interest, your cooperation, and your understanding, such goals as outlined above are easily attainable.

CREATIVE ACTIVITIES

S	S
S	S
S	S
L	E
S	S
S	S

- ENJOYS SINGING WITH THE GROUP.
- ENJOYS LISTENING TO GOOD MUSIC.
- RESPONDS TO RHYTHMS AND MUSIC.
- ENJOYS EXPRESSING HIMSELF WITH ART MATERIALS.
- WORKS NEATLY WITH ART MATERIALS.
- SHOWS GROWTH IN CREATIVE IDEAS.

EXPLANATION OF MARKS

S — SATISFACTORY

N — NEED FOR IMPROVEMENT

I — IMPROVEMENT SHOWN

EXPLORING THE WORLD AROUND HIM

S	L
S	S

- SHOWS AN INTEREST IN THE WORLD ABOUT HIM.
- IS ABLE TO PARTICIPATE IN AND UNDERSTAND SIMPLE EXPERIMENTS.

CHILDREN IN MY CLASS

Dramatic Circus Production — Johncie Flannagan Carlson, Diddy Flannagan's daughter, has head turned to make sure all students are in line.

THE GRADUATING CLASS OF 1965

Recent graduates of the Hopewell School of Childhood Kindergarten were awarded diplomas at the 16th Annual Commencement exercises at Patrick Copeland School. They are Jeanette Bates, Kathleen Bellefontaine, Kimberly Calos, Ann Easterling, Jan Harrison, Pamela Hazelwood, Robin Hobeck, Margaret Holt, Ellen McCullen, Frances Neblett, Leslie Show, Karen Stevens, Sallie Wagner, Susan Wawner. Elizabeth Weston, Barbara Youngblood and Dianne Vanko. Also Bruce Baber, Gerald Bell, Edward Bohlig, Kirk Cruppenink, Edward Dulin, James Elliott, Ray Garfinkel, Robert Hamilton, Larry Hash, William Henry, Jerrell Nickerson, Hobart Nicholson, Alan Skinner and Kenneth Swanson. Mrs. William Traylor was directress of the class and Mrs. Donald Flack was the teacher. The program presented by the children at the exercises was coordinated by Mrs. Allen Flannagan and Mrs. William Dalton was program pianist.

(Alvin J. ___ Photo

1965—Recent graduates of the Hopewell School of Childhood Kindergarten were awarded diplomas at the 16th Annual Commencement exercises at Patrick Copeland School. They are; Jeanette Bates, Kathleen Bellefontaine, Kimberly Calos, Ann Easterling, Jan Harrison, Pamela Hazewood, Robin Hobeck, Margaret Holt, Ellen McCullen, Frances Nesbett, Leslie Show, Karen Stevens, Sallie Wagner, Susan Warner, Elizabeth Weston, Barbara Youngblood, Dianne Varko, Bruce Baber, Gerald Beil, Edward Bohlig, Kirk Cruppenink, Edward Dulin, James Elliott, Ray Garfinkel, Robert Hamilton, Larry Hash, William Henry, Jerrell Nickerson, Hobart Nicholson, Alan Skinner and Kenneth Swanson, Mrs. William Traylor was directress of the class and Mrs. Donald Flack was the teacher. The program presented by the children at the exercises was coordinated by Mrs. Allen Flannagan and Mrs. William Dalton were program pianist.

1966

Kimberly Ann Calos as
"Mary Poppins"

School of Childhood Invites Pupils, Parents To Open House

This year the school bell will ring early for nursery and kindergarten children at the Hopewell School of Childhood, 519 Appomattox Street.

An open house will be held August 20 form 9a.m. to 12:30 p.m. for children and their parents to become acquainted with the school and with each other.

The nursery curriculum taught by the director, Mrs. William E. Traylor, consists of music and rhythms, stories, games, handcrafts and dramatics.

Good social behavior is emphasized and many of the three and four year olds have their first taste of sharing and organized play, good practice for the more formal situation they will encounter in a Kindergarten class.

The Kindergarten taught by Mrs. Donald Flack, is open only to children who will be attending first grade in September, 1966.

The curriculum provides an introduction to the fundamental concepts of numbers and to the vocabulary necessary for verbalizing these concepts, base phonics is preparation for reading, and special listening games which include language arts, history, social studies and science.

The children also take field trips, along to a primary book club and take a weekly newspaper.

Hopewell School of Childhood is licensed by the state of Virginia for day care, and many of the children stay to have a hot lunch and a nap, followed by supervised recreation in the afternoon.

Further information may be obtained by calling Mrs. Traylor.

Donna Joy Dail, Jasmer Kyle Rusnak, Angel Teaonna Smith, Toy Marie Spatig, Leslie Robin Whitehead, Kimberly James, Jennifer Lydia Lyman, Margaret Ann Joyner, Donna Lynn Williams, Thomas Murphey Batchelor III, Vance Massey Boss, Carter Burwell Bowyer, Douglas Dwain Brown, William Carlton Bryant, Mark Allen Dillingham, Scott Gregory Evans, John William Marshall III, Conway Faison Savage, John Wesley Spain, Jr., Robert Murray Winne, Jr.

HOPEWELL SCHOOL OF CHILDHOOD

SEVENTEETH ANNUAL COMMENCEMENT

Presenting

THE GRADUATING CLASS OF 1966

KINDERGARTEN

Friday, May 27, 1966, at 7:30 P.M.

Patrick Copeland School

Hopewell, Virginia

A VISIT TO THE WISE OLD OWL

(Cast)

Mary..Angel Smith
Bo Beep..Kimberly James
Bell Ringer....................................Carter Burwell Bowyer
Owl...Mark Dillingham
Boy...Conway Savage
Farmer...Bobby Winne
Jack..Douglas Brown
Jill...Jennifer Lyman
Yankee Doodle.................................Scott Evans
Polly...Jasmer Rusnak
Suky...Leslie Whitehead
Clown ....Vance Bose
Baa Black Sheep...............................Wesley Spain
Girl..Toy Spatig
Humpty Dumpty...............................Carl Bryant
Boy Blue.......................................Carter Burwell Bowyer
Spider ....John Marshall
Peas Porridge Hot............................Donna Williams
Peas Porridge Cold...........................Margaret Joyner
Jack Horner...................................Tim Batchelor
Rock—A—Bye.................................Donna Dail
Batman..Mystery Guest

AWARDING OF DIPLOMAS

Donna Joy Dail

Jasmer Kyle Rusnak

Angel Teaonna Smith

Toy Marie Spatig

Leslie Robin Whitehead

Kimberly James

Jennifer Lydia Lyman

Margaret Ann Joyner

Donna Lynn Williams

Thomas Murphey Batchelor III

Vance Massey Boss

Carter Burwell Bowyer

Douglas Dwain Brown

William Carlton Bryant

Mark Allen Dillingham

Scott Gregory Evans

John William Marshall III

Conway Faison Savage

John Wesley Spain, Jr.

Robert Murray Winne, Jr.

HSC Teachers: Mrs. Edna Shirley & Mrs. Patricia Fredrickson

1967—Graduates of Hopewell School of Childhood Kindergarten were awarded diplomas at the 18th Annual Commencement exercises:

Aldridge, Marshall
Stefan, Calos
Eleades, Elliott
Emacke, Wilson
Faisor, James
Diane, Henry
Hammer, Hal
McCaffrey, Timothy
McCullen, George
Haranek, Donald
Millis, Tracy
Winkes, William
Sadler, Mark
Carney, Nicholas
Bishop, Cynthia
Elmore, Cynthia
Gentry, Karen
Halfield, Alice
Shiatt, Cynthia
Latino, Julie
Leech, Annette
McChesney, Martina
Smith, Catriena
Satterwhite, Rebecca
Rideout, Kimberly
Poque, Shardn

Stefan Calos—Attorney-at-Law

Diane Henry Parr

1968—Graduates of Hopewell School of Childhood Kindergarten
19th Annual Commencement exercises

Bennett, Angela	Short, Ray
Boss, Balling	Sweitzer, Tama
Broaddus, Warner	Wellis, Scott
Camphell, Julia Ann	Winnie, Patricia
Dacey, Susan	Lawson, Curtis
Evans, Crystal	Bercau, Kathy
Geitb, Anne	Callins, Tommy
Hale, Brad	Creeden, Edward
Kaplan, Rose	Gilse, Kimberly
Latino, Robert	Yerky, John
Lecair, John	Hale, Debra
Morris, Wendy Sue	Stallard, Kathryn
Seavey, George	Ross, Katherine

PROGRAM
Pandora And The Toy Box
(Cast of Characters)

Pandora................Crystal Evens
Mother Goose..........Kimberly Giese
Peter Pumpkin..........George Seavey
Mrs. Pumpkin...........Windy Morris
Jack.....................Edward Creedon
Jill.......................Angela Bennett
Blue Boy................Brad Hale
Polly....................Kathy Bercan
Suky....................Debra Hale
Mary....................Anne Geib
Jack Nimble.............Buddy Lawson
Mary Contrary..........Kathryn Stallard
Muffin Man.............Warner Broaddus
Bow Peep...............Julie Campbell
Farmer...................Bobby Latino
Pease Porridge Hot......Susan Dacey
Pease Porridge Cold....Heather Butchinson
Yankee Doodle..........Scott Willis
Where Oh Where.......Tama Weitzer
Black Sheep.............John Yerby
Miss Muffet.............Patti Winne
Spider...................Boland Boss
Indian...................Bruce Bradshaw
Twinkle Star...........Tommy Collins
Rock-A-Bye...........Kathryn Ross

Annette leech Irby-67

1969—Bradford Dalton, B.S. Virginia Technical Institute – Teacher

1969— Kindergarten Graduation Hopewell School of Childhood, 20th Annual Commencement exercises

Klutz, Karen, McCheancy, Mark, Boyette, Stacey Morris, Billy Newman, Bobby Grainger, Myra Seacat, Steven Mitchell, Mitch Hutchinson, HiacherSusan, Elrad Hale, Missy Pugh, Ronnie Henry, Diane Townes, Bruce Elizabeth, Brochwell Newlin, Jim Youngblood, Pat Jones, Randy Lewis, Howard Partin, Allen Gates, Mason Satterfield, Gary Daniels, Jay Lonin, Carson Willett, Angelia Demin, Partier Damian.

1970—Kindergarten Graduation Hopewell School of Childhood; 21 Annual Commencement exercises

Nursery Only— Elmom Duff, Ronnie Hatch, Carminia Ovtz, Brian Shoemaker, David Roberts, George Eliades, Lori Lewis, John Doulis, Crystal Tidewell, Greg Deness, Jeffry Utz, Mark Ellen, Timmy McCume, Lisa Smith, Mark Clark, Craig Lewis, Booby Knott.

Kindergarten— Tamera Cormany, Linda Fagg, Edith Gillenwater, Tonya McCammon, Kelly McDonald, Sherry Rae Milburn, Nancy Montana, Karen Pruden, Lisa Smith, Crystal Tidwell, Tracey Wheeler, Tammy Winegar, Douglas Davidson, John Doulis, Joseph Duncan, Mark Ellis, Ronald Hatch, Marvin Humphries, James Minchew, James Roberts, Floyd Temple, Glenn Shannon.

Mrs. Sally Carwile and Martha Sue Pace–**1968**

Mrs. Sally Carwile's Nursery Class—**1970**

Mrs. Flannagan—**1970**

Mrs. Flannagan—**1972**

HOPEWELL SCHOOL OF CHILDHOOD
TWENTY—SECOND ANNUAL COMMENCEMENT

Presenting

THE GRADUATING CLASS OF 1971

KINDERGARTEN

Friday, May 21, 1971 - 7:00 P. M.

Patrick Copeland School

Hopewell, Virginia

CLASS PROGRAM

"Mrs. Pumpkin's Little Problems"

Cast

Mr. Pumpkin...Jim Minchew
Mrs. Pumpkin..Nancy Montana
Miss Mufet..Tami Cormany
Spider...Ronald Hatch
Where—O—Where...................................Jimmie Roberts
Farmer..Mike Davidson
Mary Contrary.......................................Tammy Winegar
Jack...Malcolm Barbee
Jill...Vivian Blevins
 Muffin Man...Jody Buncan
Mary Lamb..Sherry Milburn
Humpty Dumpty.......................................John Doulis

Bo Beep	Edith Gillenwater
Baa Black Sheep	Floyd Temple
Jack—Be—Nimble	Mark Ellis
Indian	Glenn Shannon
Peas Porridge Hot	Charlene Woolridge
Peas Porridge Cold	Lisa Smith
Boy Blue	Christian Lewis
Polly	Karen Pruden
Suky	Crystal Tidwell
Rock –A—Bye	Tonya McCommon

GRADUATING CLASS OF 1971
AWARDING OF DIPLOMAS

Tamera Marie Cormany

Tonya Leigh McCammon

Edith Gail Gillenwater

Sherry Rae Milburn

Karen Ann Pruden

Lisa Gayle Smith

Crystal gene Tidwell

Tammy Lynn Winegar

Vivian May Blevins

Nancy Carol Montana

Lois Charlene Woolridge

Malcolm Francis Barbee

Douglas Michael Davidson

John Paul Doulis

Joseph Conwell Duncan

Mark David Ellis

Ronald Eugene Hatch

James Meritte Minchew

James Joel Roberts

Floyd Winfield Temple III

Glenn Patrick Shannon

Mrs. Sue Pace Traylor and Mrs. Mccammon and
Mrs. Carwile.—**1972** Kindergarten & Nursery:

Lorie Leivis, Pam Leashuter, Darrin Bennett, Richard Gaglairdor, Kenneth Latino, Lisa
Morris, Kathy Sutherland, Suzane Powroznick, Mandy Thomas, Mark Clark, Daniele Dinor,
Darryl Heinplies, Donna Marlone, Luke Palmer, Eleanor Swelland, Tray Sputnig, Charlene
Woolridge, Andrea Pritchard, Ashley Enochs, Laura Jones, Melisa Moody, Charles Penir,
Bryan Tounes, Roy & Tray Swinford,.

Mrs. Vonnie West—**1973**

Ricky Birchett, Rodney Brooks, Kim Chaplin, Thomas Cormany, Tammy Durrat, Deidra Frush, Linda George, Gorden Griggs, Sharon Hatch, Jamie Jones, Tyler Koren, Rebecca Learned, Michael lowe, Long Xuan Nghiem, Jenny Noel, Lisa Norris, Rea Maria Papanico-laov, Eric Pyle, Stacy Ratliff, Beth Riddle, Nancy Vaughan, Andy West, Troy Williamson, Lori Brady, Brain Braswell.

Santa Visits Kindergarten

Jamie Lynn Jones tells Santa what's she's hoping he will bring to her house on Christmas Eve at the Christmas Party held Friday at Hopewell School of Childhood on Appomattox Street for Nursery school and Kindergarten youngsters. Jamie is the daughter of James B. Jones Jr. of 1010 North Avenue.

HOPEWELL SCHOOL OF CHILDHOOD

CLASS PROGRAM—1973
"THE WISE OLD OWL"

Twenty—Forth Annual Commencement

Patrick Copland School

Cast:

Owl...................Tyler Koren
Sect....................Sharon Hatch
Jack...................Rodney Brooks
Jill....................Deidra Ann Frush
Bo Peep..............Nancy Vaughan
Peter Pumpkin.......Andy West
Mrs. Pumpkin........Kimberly Chaplin
Miss Muffet..........Jenny Noel
Spider.................Troy Williamson
Farmer................Eric Pyles
Farmer's Wife........Rea Maria Papanicolaov
Mary Contrary.......Stacey Ratliff
Humpty Dumpty.....Long Nghiem
Yankee Doodle......Ricky Birchett
Polly..................Rebecca Learned
Suky...................Laurie Brady
Muffin Man...........Gordon Griggs
Indian..................Tom Cormany
Mary..................Lisa Norris
Peas Porridge Hot....Beth Riddle
Where oh Where......Jamie Jones
Jack-Be-Nimble......Mike Lowe
Rock-A-Bye..........Linda George

GRADUATING CLASS OF 1973

Laurie Brady
Richard Gary Birchett
Rodney Allen Brooks
Kimberly Dawn Chaplin
Thomas Marshall Cormany
Diedra Ann Frush
Linda Irene George
Gordon Wayne Griggs
Sharon Lynn Hatch
Jamie Lynn Jones
William Tyler Koren
Rebecca Anne Learned

Awarding of Diplomas

Michael Brian Lowe
Long Xuan Nghiem
Jeanette Melissa Noel
Lisa Carol Norris
Rea Maria Papanicolaov
Donald Eric Pyles
Stacey Renee' Ratliff
Beth Ann Riddle
Nancy Marie Vaughan
Andrew Armstrong West
Troy Scott Williamson

Mrs. Edwina Moore Daniel—1975

Mrs. Edwina Moore Daniel, former Mrs. Pace student, shared this teaching story about how important it was for children to experience farming that was once the chief way of life in nearly every country. Mrs. Daniel taught her children the history of American families who lived on small farms to strengthen their knowledge. As I have mentioned before, just like grandmother Pace, Mother's teachers continued to arrange many school field trips to all types of prominent Hopewell businesses as the pictures show. Mrs. Daniel along with husband Jack Daniel, Hopewell High School's Activities Director, escorted Mother's children to their farm in Prince George. The children were exposed to where they raised hogs, cattle, sheep, chickens, and planted corn, fruits, garden vegetables, hay, and wheat to explore or question and perceive life's living fields of knowledge and experiences. People cannot live without food, and nearly all our food comes from crops and animals raised on farms. Farming still remains the most important occupation in the world.

Mrs. Daniel told me the story of how one of her children was fidgety, squirmy and hypertensive and quickly informed him that, "you must have ants in your pants." Well, immediately she realized that he might have taken her seriously, so she told him that she was just kidding about the "ants being in his pants." The little boy said, "yes maim, I understand Mrs. Daniel."

Hopewell School of Childhood

Many Graduation & Play production programs, pictures and student names were lost in a large flood from 1974– 1985 .

HOPEWELL SCHOOL OF CHILDHOOD

TWENTY EIGHT ANNUAL COMMENCEMENT

PRESENTING

THE GRADUATING CLASS OF 1977

KINDERGARTEN
AND
NURSERY

FRIDAY, MAY 20, 1977—7:00 P.M.

PATRICK COPELAND SCHOOL

HOPEWELL, VIRGINIA

DIRECTOR OF SCHOOL—MRS. WM. E. TRAYLOR

KINDERGARTEN TEACHER— MRS. ALLEN FLANNAGAN

NURSERY TEACHERS—MRS. JOHN CARWILE
MRS. CHARLES MYERS

Left to Right— Sue Traylor, Sally Carwile, Donna Myers, Pat Frederickson, and Dr. Yi – Nan Chou MD daughters Jeanne & Elaine

Kindergarten Teacher-Ellen Grace Brame Garvin
Wesleyan College 1972—1976
September 1977-1986

Mrs. Sally Carwile directing the children at Patrick Copland School

A final dramatic play production by the Hopewell School of Childhood in 1985.
"Peter Pan" The Thirty—Sixth Annual Commencement

Mrs. Charles Myers

Mother reading to students on trip to farm

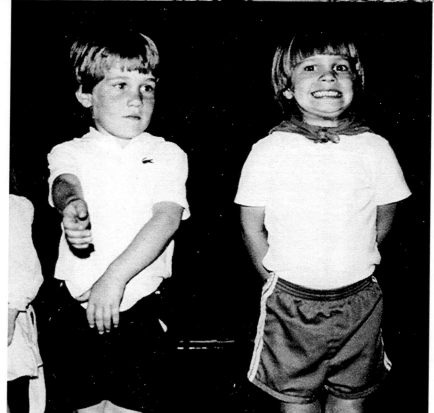

Mrs. Pace's three grandchildren October 2004:
Thompson Gardenhire Pace, III., William Ellsworth Traylor, Jr.,
Robert Pace Traylor

Thompson Gardenhire Pace III, Mrs. Pace's pioneering philosophy inspired her first grandson's, life's work.

Consultant/Owner of TGP Environmental—Tom established TGP Environmental, an environmental Service consulting firm—specializing in emissions in gratifying studies for particulate matter in 2009.

Tom worked for the Environmental Protection-Agency (EPA) for thirty-five years, where he had a variety of projects to support the EPA's missions.

He specialized in emissions characterization, strategic planning and staff development and in providing expertise in technical and policy aspects of particulate matter in the ambient air. His areas of specialization include source emissions characterization, identifying sources of air pollution that contribute to high air concentrations and poor visibility and strategies to reduce ambient concentrations. He has experience in receptor modeling, emissions inventories, transport and removal processes, ambient measurements, chemical tracers of convenience, chemical composition of source emissions and SIP development. He worked with Pharmacies 2.5, PM10, Coarse PM, Lead, Ammonia, VOC's, NOx, SO2, Elemental and Organic Carbon, Hazardous Air Pollutants, Climate Forcing Pollutants and worked directly with air quality staff in all 50 States and more than 10 countries. Fellow Member Emeritus of the Air and Waste Management Association and a registered engineer in North Carolina.

Tom is a Graduate of North Carolina State University, MSE,
Mechanical Engineering – 1978
Virginia Polytechnic Institute -1969 B.S. Mechanical Engineering

William Ellsworth Traylor, Jr.

Grandmother's second grandson, my brother, a futurist is William Ellsworth Traylor, Jr., a (R.R.T.) Registered Respiratory Therapist. Associates Degree from Mount Olive College in Science. William gained a Teachers Certificate from J. Sergeant Reynolds Community College to teach Respiratory Therapy in 1976 and became a teacher for ATI Career Training Center in Ft. Lauderdale, Florida-1989.

In 1978 Bill and his partners, Dr. Joseph Villseck, Ph.D., M.D. and Steve Rosenbloom, (R.R.T.) created the largest home healthcare company in the State of Virginia called "Virginia Cardio Pulmonary Home Care, Inc." Their nine stores were called "The Recovery Room." Bill and partner, Steve Rosenbloom who owns "West Home Health Care, Inc.," that originated as a subsidiary of VCPHC, had 3,500 patients, a staff of (RN) Registered Nurses, (L.P.N.) License Practical Nurses, (E.M.T.), Emergency Medical Technicians, (R.R.T.) Registered Respiratory Therapist, (C.R.T.T.) Certified Respiratory Therapist, directors and store managers. The company was acquired by Foster Medical in 1987.

Virginia Cardio Pulmonary Home Care

Serving all of Virginia with 24-hour service

P.O. Box 9756 ● Richmond, Virginia 23228
Phone (804) 276-0787 ● Toll free 1-800-552-3712

Bill Traylor, President

Steve Rosenbloom,
Vice President

RECOVERY ROOM REPORT:

The Recovery Room had nine offices across Virginia and in Princeton, West Virginia to help you with your home health care needs.

The corporate office and billing department were located at:

Virginia Cardio Pulmonary Home Care, Inc.

P.O. Box 9756
8403 Sanford Drive
Richmond, Virginia 23228
(804) 226-9407

With Satellite office at:
801 E. High Street Suite D
Charlottesville, Virginia 22901

VA CARDIO-PULMONARY HOME CARE INC.
STATEMENT OF FINANCIAL POSITION
JUL 31.1984
SEE ACCOUNTANT'S COMPILATION REPORT

ASSETS

CURRENT ASSETS:

Cash on Hand and in Banks	889.06	
Investments	199,365.55	
Note Receivable Subsidiaries	86,864.65	
Accounts Receivable (Net)	684,079.00	
Inventory	153,053.27	
Loans To Stockholders	20,069.94	
Other Current Assets	29,558.76	
		1,173,880.23

FIXED ASSETS:

Furniture,Fixtures & Equipment	1,189,709.59	
Transportation Equipment	178,357.33	
Leasehold Improvements	19,075.06	
Less Accumulated Depreciation	643,221.82	
		743,920.16

OTHER ASSETS:

Organization Expense (Net)	30.00	
Cash Value - Life Ins	6,269.02	
		6,299.02
TOTAL ASSETS		1,924,099.41

LIABILITIES & STOCKHOLDERS EQUITY

CURRENT LIABILITIES:

Accounts Payable	215,437.59	
Accrued Expenses	646.06	
Income Taxes Payable	210.00	
Excess Losses of Subsidiaries	50,893.70	
Loans From Stockholders	9,563.08	
Notes Payable	322,884.99	
Other Current Liabilites	1,780.94	
		601,416.36

LONG TERM LIABILITIES:

Notes Payable	366,533.80	
Deferred Income Taxes	186,849.00	
CSV Life Insurance Loan	5,195.27	
		558,578.07

STOCKHOLDERS' EQUITY:

Capital Stock Issued & O/S		1,500.00	
Capital in Excess of Par		18,290.49	
Treasury Stock		75,489.64-	
Retained Earnings - Beginning	521,643.25		
Current Profit or Loss-	298,160.88		
Retained Earnings - Ending		819,804.13	
			764,104.98
TOTAL LIAB. & EQUITY			1,924,099.41

My brother has a very keen business mind, like my father. His company achieved financial independence, and created many jobs for others who also became financially independent because of their association with his company.

He is one truly special person, special far beyond my ability to express in words. One of the most positive people I've ever know. He is such a good person, tough and resilient, but soft and compassionate, and not too proud to change when he thinks he should. A good friend, loyal and loving, inspires me greatly in all the important decisions of my life. He has a heart of gold. I've never know anyone with such a tender, yet indomitable spirit.

He helped me shape my ideas when I was growing up. He played a part in my destiny. He taught me to reach for the sky when I might have been satisfied with the ground. He helped me to develop confidence in myself and made me feel I could do anything. He has been a real-life example to me of how never to give up in the face of disappointment, fear, conflict, and trouble.

My life would have been very different without his example, and my days wouldn't be as joyful without his love.

Robert Pace Traylor, Mrs. Pace's third Grandson

Grandmother's and Mother's words and lessons are carried out and fixed in my life travels today. Atlantic Christian College-Barton, Wilson, North Carolina, M. Ed. Graduate Course Studies; Bachelors in Graphic Arts Education/Theater Drama NK-12 License teacher; 1974-1979. Continued to advance studies to acquire an Associate Degree, as a License Practical Nurse. I am about to further my education journey, to acquire a Registered Nurse Degree. I know that there's something deep inside that helps us become what we can. Never underestimate the power of your actions, past or present. With one small gesture you can change a person's life. God puts us all in each other's lives to impact one another in some way, and today, I look for God in others.

If I have done one thing right in my life, I've always found successful mentors to guide me. People ask me how I am able to accomplish so much, and I tell them, it's all due to the quality of my mentors. My brother and Steve Rosenbloom were and still are my greatest mentors. According to one article I read, you can determine the income of an individual by adding up and averaging the incomes of his or her ten best friends. This is how I am able to see beyond my problems by accepting to know someone who has a higher perspective.

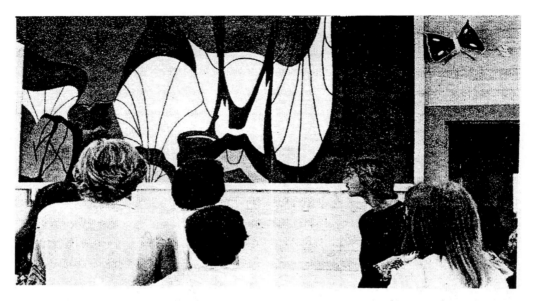

Robert Traylor Mural Viewed

ACC Art Students Assist
Caswell's Mural Project

Caswell Developmental Center
NC Division of State Operated Healthcare Facilities

In 1976, as an Art Education Student at Atlantic Christian College, Robert Pace Traylor designed an abstract bicycle mural that was unconditionally selected by the North Carolina State Arts Curator and placed in the non-ambulatory special project Museum and Visitors Center at Caswell Development Center.

Information Technology Web Designer as owner/operator Internet Service Provider (ISP) for companies since 1984; Trivibot, Inc., Pace-Net Marketing Associates, Inc., Edna's Effanbee Doll Company, Inc., the First Internet Effanbee Doll Company. Network design infrastructures can be observed in the following uniform resource locators (URL's): www.whhci.com, www.effnbeedolls.com, www.fumchopewell.org, www.meditrade.com, www.pacekindergarten.com, and www.vatraincollectors.com.

In 1980, one year after leaving Atlantic Christian College in Wilson, North Carolina I returned home to work as Assistant Manager for The Country Club of Virginia, Inc. when my brother Bill asked if I would like to join his work force at VCPHC in management as one of his executive officers. I told him, I knew country club management and teacher education skills but nothing about respiratory, medical supplies or healthcare. He said, "I'm President, I'm a pulmonary teacher, have taught cardio pulmonary and respiratory course studies at J. Sergeant Reynolds. It's a service, just like public schools and country club management, and I have nothing to say except EXCELLENCE will reign here. I will teach you the medical care service skills necessary. I will hold you to high standards. I will support you, demand from you and yes, castrate you when you don't come up to snuff."

Virginia Cardio Pulmonary's patient care services were impeccable and the reason we were the largest Home Health Care Company in Virginia, just like West Home Health Care, Inc. is today is due to excellence in patient care. We were involved in many community service affairs and worked together with local business officials for reinforcement.

I asked my brother, "Where was my office going to be located in his nice new corporate facility on Sanford Road off Stables Mill in Richmond," and he said, "the warehouse." I said, "What?" I am a teacher, county club manager have dinned with Governor John and Eddie Dalton, with entrepreneur congress members and the distinguished editor from the Richmond Times Dispatch, Virginus Dabney and you are going to put me in the warehouse?" He said, "How are you going to learn all the (DME), Durable Medical Equipment, respiratory and medical supplies if not to start in the warehouse where they are?" I told him, "well, if that's so, you are going to build me an air conditioned office," and so he did.

My personal work philosophy is to finish every day and be done with it. You have done what you could. Some blunders and absurdities no doubt have crept in; forget them as soon as you can. Tomorrow is a new day; begin it well and serenely and with too high a spirit to be cumbered with your old nonsense. This day is all that is good and fair. It is too dear, with its homes and invitations, to waste a moment on yesterdays.

This was at the Department of Education with Governor now Senator Mark Warner
and my best friend Ed Damerel, Television Specialist.

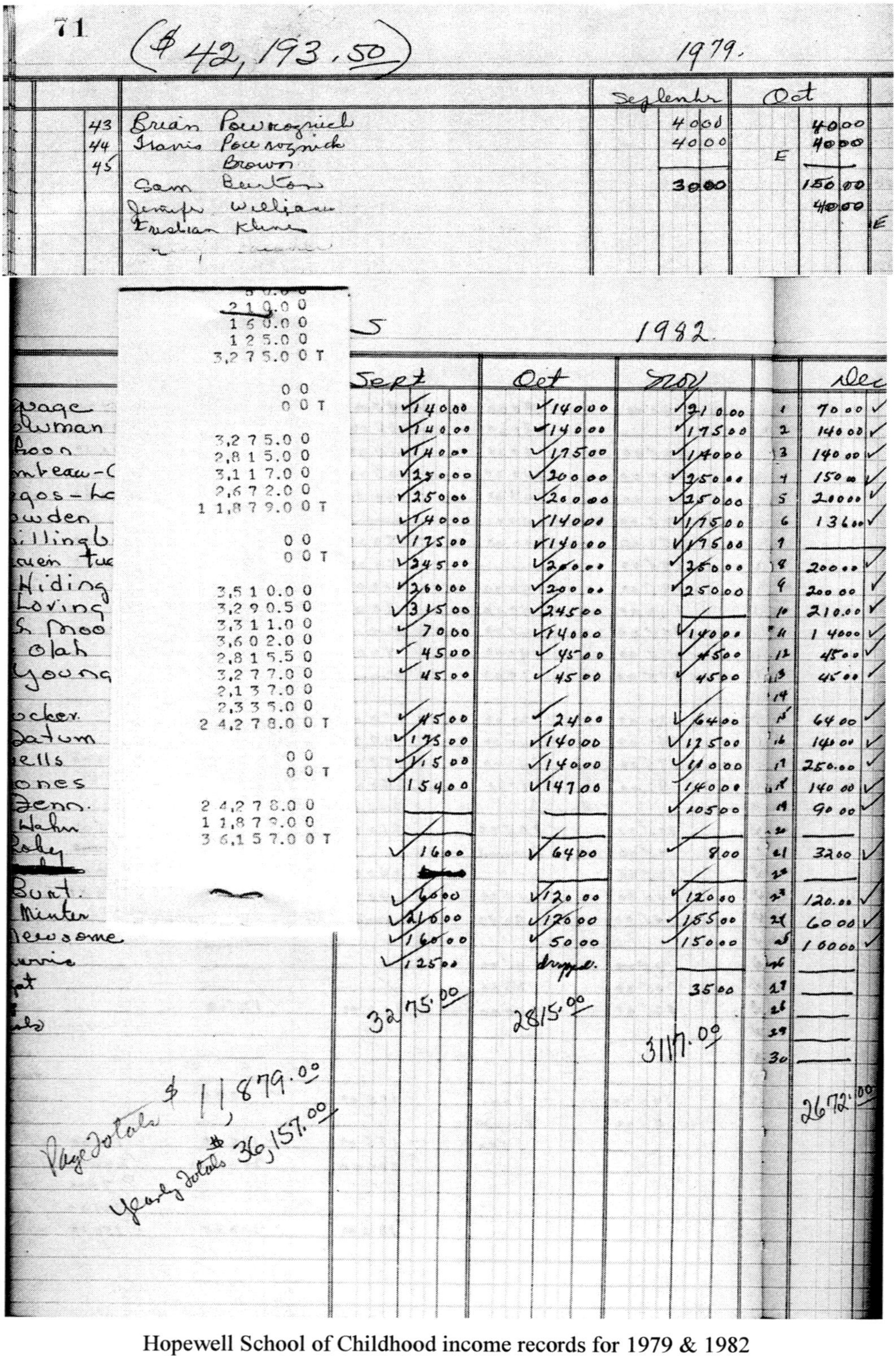
71
($42,193.50)
1979.
Septenber
Oct
43 Brian Powrozynick 40.00 40.00
44 Travis Powrozynick 40.00 40.00
45 Brown E
Sam Burton 30.00 150.00
Jennifer Williams 40.00
Christian Kline E
210.00
160.00
125.00
3,275.00 T
0 0
0 0 T
3,275.00
2,815.00
3,117.00
2,672.00
11,879.00 T
0 0
0 0 T
3,510.00
3,290.50
3,311.00
3,602.00
2,815.50
3,277.00
2,137.00
2,335.00
24,278.00 T
0 0
0 0 T
24,278.00
11,879.00
36,157.00 T
1982.
Sept
Oct
Nov
Dec
3275.00
2815.00
3117.00
2672.00
Page Totals $ 11,879.00
Yearly Totals $ 36,157.00

Hopewell School of Childhood income records for 1979 & 1982

William Ellsworth Traylor Sr., 75, of Hopewell, passed away October 8, 1991, in Henrico Doctors Hospital, Richmond, following a brief illness.

He was born in Ettrick, was the son of the late Edward Marvin and Hazel Monroe Traylor, had been a lifelong resident of the area and was a member of the First United Methodist Church.

He was a honored veteran of World War II, having served as Staff Sergeant with the U.S. (AAF) Army Air Corps., as Medical Administrative Surgical Specialist.

Graduate of University of Richmond in Business Administration June 4th, 1956.

Bill Traylor was a senior purchasing agent for Allied-Signal Corporation for thirty -five years, retired in 1981, a member of the Hopewell Rotary Club, "SCORE" Senior Citizens Of Retired Executives, and the Kelly Class of First United Methodist Church.

He is survived by his wife, Martha Sue Pace Traylor of this city; son, William Ellsworth Traylor Jr., Robert Pace Traylor and daughter-in-law, Edna Marie Traylor, all of Hopewell; a brother Daniel Traylor N. St. Petersburg, Florida, two grandchildren, Lorraine Wesler, Richard Mahone.

October 1991, I wrote this poem for my father who inspired excellent leadership in my life's travels.

I searched my heart
the whole day through
to find the perfect
words for you.

The words describing you
were difficult to compose,
for your true nature was
hard to disclose.

As a private man with insight
and intelligence to share,
you extended your hand
while saying, "I Care."

A generosity of humor
was your greatest gift,
when talking about Bear
and sometimes, Tiff.

We talked about how life
was so full of games,
before we departed
to play with the trains.

Of all the people I have met
in life's daily chores,
your wisdom and grace excels
and was rightfully yours.

Your variable knowledge
of music, electronics, business
and even medicine,
would impress even the brightest scholars
from Newton to Edison.

And though distance
did separate us at times,
our love did swell,
as the seeds were embedded
and embedded well.

Time cannot be exchanged
neither be bought,
and for those who love
time is not.

We are all more than
the sum of our parts,
but, remembrance of you Dad,
will lie deep in my heart.

Just remember Dad that you
were God's special child,
He walks with you now
equally proud.

Show Him the way
as you did me,
and He'll show you the truth
that will set you free.

So, till I can come
where you will be,
I'll sort of watch over
Bill and Mom for thee.

This I can do
with the gentlest of hands,
without interrupting
any of God's plans.

So you rest, you rest easy
my Dad,

Your worries are none,
for you can be assured today
that thy will has been done,
Thy will has been done.

Love, Bobby

My father was a gracious host to all. To his family and friends, he leaves the precious gifts of a great sense of humor and finding simple joy in a good joke. He was gifted in numerous skills and was an inspiration to many. He had a passion for life, helping and giving to others. Father will be remembered by the public for his generosity and business savvy, but those closest to him will remember his sense of humor. He was a pretty sharp guy. My brother and I both learned about business from him.

My father was not only a man of tremendous intellect, but of conscience, caring, dedication, and faith. Among the worst periods of my life was the year 1991, marked by the passing of my father at age 75. Like many of my peers, I realized too late in life he was one of a generation of extraordinary American men who grew up during the Great Depression, fought and won a World War, and returned home to take his place in the workforce responsible for building the American nation. During the Great Depression he loved photography and radio. He couldn't afford a projector or radio, so he bought the parts and built them. In the slide Projector were two large magnifier glasses to reverse polarity for projection. He used non flammable asbestos lining in his wooden box. I still have many of his creative, unique and ingeniously built radio and the slide projector.

My father was selfless and really wanted nothing more than for his children to have a better life than he. From, Father I inherited perseverance and Mother the same, but to always do things correctly.

GENERAL FITNESS

Taking into account the above statements and also other observable evidence of suitability, what is your overall estimate of the chances that this candidate will be an efficient officer and a credit to the service.

| Not Recommended | : Recommended : with hesitancy : | : Recommended : | : Recommended : with confidence | : Recommended : with enthusiasm |

General remarks: *Good material for an officer*

William F Martin
NAME
Lt. Col. Chief
RANK
Surgical Service
Sedgley + Field Va

Martha Sue Pace Traylor, *83, of Appomattox Street Hopewell, died Monday, October 13, 2003, in John Randolph Medical Center.*

Mrs. Traylor was born in New London, N.C. and had been a resident of this area since 1925. She was a graduate of Hopewell High School in 1938 with Academic Course study in French Circle, Vice-President '34, Edgar Allan Poe Literary Society; Athletic Association; Mock Minstrel School News Staff. She was a member of First United Methodist Church, United Methodist Women's Club, Helping Hands, Circle and was the former owner of Hopewell's First Day Care Center, "The Hopewell School of Childhood.

She was the daughter of the late Thompson Gardenhire Pace Sr. and Patricia Louise Ross Pace, and widow of William Ellsworth Traylor Sr.

Mrs. Traylor is survived by two sons, William Ellsworth Traylor Jr. of Del-Ray Beach, Florida and Robert Pace Traylor and his wife Edna, of Hopewell; two grandchildren, Richard C. Mahon of Cumberland, Va., and Lorraine Wesler of ID., along with six great grandchildren, Keith White, Chris Mahon, Randal Mahon, Tommy Wesler, Timothy James Wesler, and Lindsey Wesler.

SEPARATION QUALIFICATION RECORD

SAVE THIS FORM. IT WILL NOT BE REPLACED IF LOST

This record of job assignments and special training received in the Army is furnished to the soldier when he leaves the service. In its preparation, information is taken from available Army records and supplemented by personal interview. The information about civilian education and work experience is based on the individual's own statements. The veteran may present this document to former employers, prospective employers, representatives of schools or colleges, or use it in any other way that may prove beneficial to him.

1. LAST NAME—FIRST NAME—MIDDLE INITIAL			MILITARY OCCUPATIONAL ASSIGNMENTS		
TRAYLOR, WILLIAM E.			10. MONTHS	11. GRADE	12. MILITARY OCCUPATIONAL SPECIALTY
2. ARMY SERIAL No.	3. GRADE	4. SOCIAL SECURITY No.	2	Pvt	Medical Basic Training (657)
33 132 156	Sgt		24	Cpl	Surgical Technician (861)
5. PERMANENT MAILING ADDRESS *(Street, City, County, State)*			4	Sgt	Radiology Technician (AAF) (264)
408 Wyth Street Petersburg, Dinwiddie County, Virginia			12	Sgt	Medical Administrative Specialist (AAF) (673)
6. DATE OF ENTRY INTO ACTIVE SERVICE	7. DATE OF SEPARATION	8. DATE OF BIRTH			
10 Feb 1942	1 Oct 1945	23 Apr 1916			
9. PLACE OF SEPARATION					
Separation Center, Ft. Geo. G. Meade, Md.					

SUMMARY OF MILITARY OCCUPATIONS

13. TITLE—DESCRIPTION—RELATED CIVILIAN OCCUPATION

<u>MEDICAL ADMINISTRATIVE SPECIALIST (AAF)</u>--Acted as Flight Surgeon's assistant in AAF Fighter Group sick quarters. Supervised personnel of unit in administration, care and treatment of sick, injured and wounded. Supervised requisitioning of medical supplies. Assisted Flight Surgeon in instructing Medical enlisted personnel in first aid, nursing and sterilization. Coordinated preparation of Medical records and reports. Operated field flouroscopic equipment.

<u>RELATED CIVILIAN OCCUPATION</u>--Chief Clerk.

Mr. Allen W. Flannagan, Mrs. Martha Sue Pace Traylor and
Mrs. Virginia (Diddy) Ford Flannagan

CITY OF HOPEWELL
300 NORTH MAIN STREET, HOPEWELL, VIRGINIA 23860
PHONE: 804.541.2220 FAX: 804.541.2318

PETITION TO CHANGE STREET NAME

1. Petitioner(s Name: <u>Robert Pace Traylor</u>

Petitioner(s Address: <u>519 Appomattox Street Hopewell, Virginia 23860</u>

Daytime Phone: <u>(804) 458-0735</u>

Email Address: <u>rpt-emt@verizon.net</u>

2. Current Street Name and Route Number (if applicable): <u>Madison</u>

3. Proposed Street Name: **<u>PACE STREET</u>**

4. Please describe the reason(s) why you are seeking the street name change:

Mrs. Pace's Kindergarten was originally located at her home 208 Ramsey Avenue in 1941, it was relocated to the Brown Apartment Building in 1948 and finally to the corner of NEW Street "PACE" and Appomattox Street from 1958 until it closed in 1986. Although Madison Street has no houses, it does have the memories of the thousands of children whose lives were enriched through Mrs. Pace's loving care.

Mrs. Pace's Kindergarten was an important part of the City of Hopewell for 45 years, from 1941 to 1986 as Hopewell's First Licensed Daycare Center. Mrs. Pace's Kindergarten contributed to the City of Hopewell and achievement to the thousands of children's day-to-day lives and of its citizen's through its teacher's love and devotion.

Hopewell City Mayor-Christina J. Luman-Bailey, William Ellsworth Traylor Jr., Robert Pace Traylor, Edna Marie Traylor standing in front of New **"PACE"** Street sign.

Proclamation

of the

City of Hopewell, Virginia

WHEREAS, "Mrs. Pace's Kindergarten" was an important part of the City of Hopewell for 45 years, 1941 to 1986, having begun at 208 Ramsey Avenue as Hopewell's First Licensed Daycare Center and later moving to Brown Apartment Building in 1948 then finally to 519 Appomattox Street; and

WHEREAS, "Mrs. Pace's Kindergarten" contributed to the City of Hopewell and the enrichment of the day to day lives of its citizens through the teachers' love and devotion to the thousands of children educated there; and

WHEREAS, "Mrs. Pace's Kindergarten" was one of the stabilizing factors that made the City and surrounding community that it served such a popular residential area; and

WHEREAS, the many services of "Mrs. Pace's Kindergarten" reached and touched the lives of many families of the City of Hopewell; and

WHEREAS, through its many community efforts, "Mrs. Pace's Kindergarten" helped to make the City of Hopewell a better place for all its citizens to live; and

WHEREAS, the Pace-Traylor family is celebrating the memory of their grandmother, Patricia Louise Pace, and wish to honor her school's 45 years of educating and caring for Hopewell children; and

WHEREAS, the Pace-Traylor family will observe a day of celebration on October 25, 2008; and

NOW, THEREFORE, BE IT RESOLVED BY THE CITY COUNCIL OF HOPEWELL that this body commends "Mrs. Pace's Kindergarten" on the occasion of the commemoration of its 45 years of service to the Hopewell families whose children were educated there and to the community it served and proclaims Saturday, October 25, 2008, as Patricia Louise Pace Day in the City of Hopewell.

BE IT FURTHER RESOLVED that the Clerk of the Council is authorized and directed to transmit an appropriate copy of this resolution to the Pace-Traylor family.

IN TESTIMONY WHEREOF, I have hereunto set my hand and caused to be affixed the Great Seal of the City of Hopewell in the Commonwealth of Virginia this 14th day of October 2008.

Brenda S. Pelham

Brenda S. Pelham, Mayor
City of Hopewell, Virginia

Chapter 10: Giving back to Hopewell Community

The following successful businesses are by former students of "Mrs. Pace's and The Hopewell School of Childhood. Her students gave back to the community before they ever left.

Once again, these businesses are from students who learned to rebuild and strengthen, as long as they lived in the Hopewell community by visiting its schools, banks, legal offices, real-estate offices, police station, fire department and the nursing home as the pictures show. They were exposed to all different types of careers and livelihoods, to explore or question, to perceive relationships between fields of knowledge and experiences. Grandmother explored different kinds of education with no oppression. By discovering and building on each child's strengths, she instilled a lifetime of enthusiasm for learning.

Grandmother and Mother unselfishly gave up their personal interest to provide leadership and guidance to community members, students, and professionals. They demonstrated how to respectfully retain cultural values, how to make informed decisions about human issues while retaining respect for other's values. You are unlikely to meet any successful person who cannot point to a teacher who played a significant, positive role in their development. This is why grandmother and grandfather left her three grandchildren an estate trust fund for future innovative education concepts.

The world's most powerful teachers perform acts of service, they take well-calculated risks, and they work everyday with passion, persistence and care. They open children's minds and hearts and the minds and hearts of other teachers. They communicate to every child that he or she has worth, and make sure that every child has access to a knowledgeable caring adult everyday. Mrs. Pace's teachers and children were FAMILY. The possibilities of a child's dreams became a reality through their efforts. Mrs. Pace helped her teachers to teach, so that knowledge was not wasted and not separated from other future experience. She sometimes remained silent, observing and absorbing the messages that children gave her. She saw the suffering of her children and she didn't pander to it.

She worked with her teachers and taught her students that suffering was erased, and future suffering was erased as a result of what they did everyday. She used personal memory of what it was like to be a child, what it was like to be a struggling teacher, in her efforts to teach her philosophy and practice. Mrs. Pace had a wonderful ministry.

And finally, grandmother realized when she transformed children's lives she was in the process of transforming herself. You do as my Grandmother did and GOD will bless you.

I thank GOD for my grandmother, Patricia Louis Ross Pace and her family's life as we reflected on a career of which she was so proud. Grandmother was given many gifts, which enabled her to give to others. I rejoice in those gifts and in the generosity to share her gifts. I pray for Mrs. Pace, that we shall remember her cherished relationships with all of us, her accommodating and supporting nature, her elegance and grace of a southern lady, her boundless generosity, kindness and thoughtfulness toward all of us with fondness and affection.

A message in my travels taught me a great truth. I already had what everyone is searching for and few ever find: The one person in the world who I was born to love forever, a person like me, who had generosity to share gifts of beloved future healthcare and education mystery.

I am a person rich in simple treasures. I live in a shelter, where l am forever home, and no trouble or even a little death can knock down this beloved school house.

The Florence Nightingale Pledge

I solemnly pledge myself before God and presence of this assembly; to pass my life in purity and to practice my profession faithfully.

I will abstain from whatever is deleterious and mischievous and will not take or knowingly administer any harmful drug.

I will do all in my power to maintain and elevate the standard of my profession and will hold in confidence all personal matters committed to my keeping and family affairs coming to my knowledge in the practice of my calling.

With loyalty will I endeavor to aid the physician in his work and devote myself to the welfare of those committed to my care.

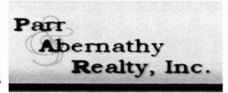

274

REFERENCES

- Du Pont

- "Thelma Olaker School of Dance."

- Galinsky, E. & Phillips, D. (1988) The day-care debate. Parents.

- Gotts, E.E. (1988). The right to quality child care. Childhood Education.

- Hofferth, S.L. (1987). Implications of family trends for children: A research perspective.

- Hopewell News Paper. (1941-1986).

- Appomattox Regional Library

- Scarr & Weinberg. (1986). The Early Childhood enterprise: Care and education of the young. American Psychologist.

- Shellenbarger, S. (1994). Companies help solve day-care problems. The Wall Street Journal, July 22, 1994.

- Reprint Quote with permission from the National Network for Child Care - NNCC.

- Boschee, M.A., & Jacobs, G. (1997). Childcare in the United States: Yesterday and today. Internet. National Network for Child Care. (www.nncc.org).

- Bridgman, A. (1989). Early Childhood Education and Childcare. Arlington, VA: American Association of School Administrators.

- Berenbeim, R. E. (1992). Corporate Programs for Early Education Improvement. Report Number 1001. New York: The Conference Board

- Caswell Center in Kinston North Carolina

- First United Methodist Church Hopewell

- Stephen Sowulewski, Associate professor of health
Reynolds Community College and Parishioner at St. Michael's Catholic Church.

- Ann Royster, (Mrs. Laura Woehr's daughter)

- Faith Farris Gable

- Johncie Flannagan

- Kim Calos

- Billy Williamson

Frequently Searched Day Care and Child Development Experts:

- Mary Ainsworth,

- Jay Belsky, Steve Biddulph, John Bowlby, T. Berry Brazelton, M.D,
  Urie Bronfrenbrenner

- Bryce Christensen, Dorothy Conniff, Dr. Peter S. Cook, Karen de Coster

- James Dobson, Wendy Dreskin, Brandon Dutcher,

- Mary Eberstadt, Amitai Etzioni,

- Joseph Farah, Don Feder, Gregory Flanagan, Isabelle Fox, Selma   Fraiberg,

- Donna Fargo

- *M.L. Genuis, Stanley Greenspan,*

- *Ronald Haskins Kathryn Hooks, Brenda Hunter,*

- *Jerome Kagan, Robert Karen, Marnie Ko,*

- *NICHD - National Institute for Child Health and Development*

- *Penelope Leach, Kathryn Jean Lopez, Norman M. Losenz, Rich Lowry,*

- *Michelle Malkin, Anne Manne, Ilana Mercer, Patricia Morgan, Bill Muehlenberg,*

- *Kate O'Beirne*

- *Kathleen Parker, Anne Pierce*

- *Brian Robertson, John Rosemond, Steven Rhoads,*

- *Phyllis Schlafly, Laura Schlessinger J. Conrad Schwartz, Thomas Shaheen,*
  Charles Siegel, Byrna Siegel,

- *Andrew Peyton Thomas,*

- *Seyla Vee*

- *Suzanne Venker*

- *Charmaine Crouse Yoest*

- *Karl Zinsmeister*

277